WONDER and WHISKEY

WONDER and WHISKEY

Insights on Faith
from the Music of Dave Matthews Band

Jeffrey A. Nelson

Foreword by Sharon Seyfarth Garner

WIPF & STOCK · Eugene, Oregon

WONDER AND WHISKEY
Insights on Faith from the Music of Dave Matthews Band

Wipf & Stock
An Imprint of Wipf and Stock Publishers
199 W. 8th Ave., Suite 3
Eugene, OR 97401

www.wipfandstock.com

PAPERBACK ISBN: 978-1-5326-4519-8
HARDCOVER ISBN: 978-1-5326-4520-4
EBOOK ISBN: 978-1-5326-4521-1

Manufactured in the U.S.A.   05/17/18

For James and Sharon,
who taught me a love of music from the beginning.

CONTENTS

FOREWORD

Music builds bridges and touches our heart and soul. It connects diverse people and invites conversation in unexpected and meaningful ways. However, in our increasingly polarized world it is harder than ever to make genuine connections. We are trapped inside our technological, ideological, and emotional silos, unwilling to step outside our comfort zone and experience authentic relationship. It is funny the way that, when you think about it, our common humanity is so easily lost among our differences.

Wonder and Whiskey is an invitation to reconnect; to use the powerful lyrics of Dave Matthews as material with which to build a bridge across the chasms that threaten to separate us. Jeff offers an honest, insightful, and thought-provoking way to come together, heal past wounds, and share the journey of faith in an exciting new way. He knows that conversation based on song lyrics offers a safe space to tackle the tough topics without immediately becoming personally vulnerable.

I've often heard life described as a tapestry. Usually, it looks like just a big mess of loose ends, knots, and random strings. However, if we take time for a closer look, this mess is being woven into a spectacular work of art. *Wonder and Whiskey* opens our eyes to see both sides of the tapestry: both the mess and the beauty of our everyday lives and of our human interconnectedness.

Dave Matthews Band embodies this fullness of the human experience. Even their jam band style is an invitation to an honest conversation between the musicians and the audience, especially during live performances, when their energy and raw humanity fill the air. Several summers ago, my family attended a DMB concert where we unexpectedly ran into Jeff and his wife. At that concert, the connection between the audience members and the musicians as they jammed was a musical breath of fresh air that drew us all together.

In the pages that follow, Jeff invites us to enjoy that fresh air, lean into our own faith experiences, and listen for new perspectives. He leads us out of our comfort zones—either of faith or music—and into a deeper exploration of our shared human experience. There is no right or wrong in the sharing of our life stories. If we can come together with open hearts and open minds, we just may discover that the world is indeed small and full of mountains and oceans and winters and rivers and stars. Enjoy the journey, crank up DMB on your speakers and invite others to join you in an authentic conversation about this beautiful mess we call life.

Sharon Seyfarth Garner

ACKNOWLEDGMENTS

Like pretty much everything else, writing a book is not a one-person endeavor. This work has many fingerprints on it, left from one step to the next, and I am grateful to them all for their contributions large and small along the way.

Thank you to Myles Werntz for the early feedback and suggestions about pitching the idea, and to Chris Spinks for passing it along once I did so. Thanks to Matthew Wimer and RaeAnne Harris for their direction in shaping everything after that.

Robert Saler provided some helpful guidance regarding the proper use of a popular band's music for a book, for which I am grateful.

Thanks to Sharon Seyfarth Garner for her words that lead everything off. I'm glad to share both a love of spirituality and of this band's music. See you at Blossom this summer.

I'm grateful to my family, who put up with me stealing time to write, as well as my grumpiness when I don't like how it's going. And always for their love and support.

And thank you to Dave, Carter, Stefan, Boyd, LeRoi, Tim, Rashawn, and Jeff. Your art has gotten me through more than you'll ever know.

1

INTRODUCTION

Like many others, I became a Dave Matthews Band fan in college. The band's core demographic from the beginning has been college-age, where songs like "Ants Marching" and "Too Much" would be played at frat parties and the local bar scene, providing the soundtrack for flirtation and libations of a young and carefree crowd still discovering their place in the world. My story of coming to fandom, however, started in a different place, and its blossoming happened in less expected ways.

I discovered the band in high school by happenstance, when sometime in 1994 I saw the music video for their first major single, "What Would You Say." The video itself is a quirky mix of avant-garde performance art and snippets from a live performance of the song. I wouldn't see the video again for a few years, but that one viewing left an impression in several ways.

First, when finally seeing it again later, I was surprised that it included the strange artistic elements. Somehow, I had forgotten or blocked out those parts of the video because I was drawn more to the footage of the band playing together. I was so struck by the amalgamation of a frontman playing acoustic guitar, a violinist, a saxophonist, and the sound of a harmonica that the other images hadn't registered in my memory. This combination of instruments and sound was such a unique find in an era where the distorted guitars and flannel shirts of what people called "grunge" still reigned, if only for a short while longer.

I bought their major label debut album *Under the Table and Dreaming* shortly after, my intrigue quickly turning to admiration. I made it a point to seek out their follow-up, *Crash*, a few years later.

Even though in those days I'd faithfully purchase each new release, liking Dave Matthews Band's music in high school was more of a casual thing. I loved their creative arrangements with an atypical array of instruments, especially given what else was considered popular at the time. But it was during my college years that several things occurred to transform my appreciation to true devotion.

I saw them live for the first time during the summer of 1999, in between my freshman and sophomore years. After hearing my stated desire to see them in concert, my then-girlfriend invited me down to see them at Riverbend Music Center in Cincinnati. While the trip was memorable for additional reasons, including getting in my first car accident, the show itself was my own discovery of what devoted fans had known for quite some time already: their live performances are the true engine of what makes this band great. The extended jams, the interplay between the members on-stage, and even Matthews's banter between songs make them an unparalleled live experience.

The second episode that solidified my fandom came while I was going through a difficult time my junior year. I was majoring in Religion, with plans to become a pastor, but a series of events that year were throwing my faith in general—let alone my career plans—into doubt. Chief among them were creeping questions related to God's existence and activity in the world for which I wasn't finding easy answers. I was facing an increased struggle to pray and to focus on my studying of theological themes, because I wondered if either were true or worth my time.

Added to the difficulty was that my expression of these doubts was causing strains between me and more conservative-minded

Christian friends, to the point where relationships began to fray and my involvement in an evangelical campus ministry was becoming increasingly unwelcome. The less I seemed to adhere to certain standards of belief, the less some people seemed to want me around. Others were sympathetic, but the negative reactions were palpable enough that they weighed heavily upon me, and having a part of my spiritual support erode in this way only added to how I wrestled with these issues.

While trying to find my way through this dark period, I did what I always do: I turned to music to help me through. I recall one afternoon when I popped my well-worn *Under the Table and Dreaming* CD into my stereo as I sat, half-numb, at my desk chair. I was paying attention just enough to hear Matthews sing reflectively while he strummed on the song "Typical Situation," where he demands loyalty and conformity from an unnamed subject and threatens consequences if they don't comply.

I heard my situation—perhaps more typical than I knew at the time—reflected in those lines. The spirit of these questions and subsequent threats were present in what I'd been hearing for months, and this song had described it so well. It was the first of many instances when I began to consider the thoughtfulness of the band's lyrics in a new way, thanks to this first moment of hearing my own life in them. It was also the first time I could hear their words' relevance to my faith, even if that connection had never been intended. I didn't know it then, but there would be many more instances to come when the music of Dave Matthews Band would help see me through a trying spiritual time.

Favorite artists differ from person to person, but music's spiritual power lies in how we are able to hear our own lives in the songs we listen to. Our own struggles, joys, triumphs, and disappointments couldn't have been known to the songwriters as they composed, but music's ability to make us feel something is in how its combination of mood and poetry transcends what was on its writer's mind and speaks into what we're going through.

Some may pick this book up and wonder why I explore the spiritual potential in Dave Matthews Band's songs. Why this band,

and why now? After all, some may argue that the group's highest point might be behind them. Songs from their more recent albums don't get the same radio play that singles from their earliest work continue to enjoy. I recall an interaction back when their album *Big Whiskey & the GrooGrux King* was released, where I mentioned on Facebook how much I liked it and a friend replied, "Oh, are they still good?"

As recently as 2016, Dave Matthews Band has remained one of the top touring musical acts for most of its twenty-five-year tenure.[1] Just as I first discovered in the summer of 1999, the experience of seeing them play in person can be far more memorable and impactful than what their studio albums convey. Both longtime fans who have remained devoted since those early years and those who have become fans since then have recognized this, which helps the band maintain a popularity that isn't dependent on album or single rankings and radio circulation. In that sense, a book on their music is as timely as ever.

But some may also wonder why anyone would want to explore themes related to faith or spirituality using this band's music. After all, one enduring stereotype of both the band and its fanbase is that their songs are geared toward an immature, party-loving demographic, good for little more than accompanying binge-drinking and other irresponsible behavior.

And yet if my afternoon experience in my room is any indication, many also find much deeper resonance with the band's songs beyond providing a party soundtrack. Some of their lyrics do touch on having a good time, but others explore themes related to belief, relationships, social justice, peace, and so much more. Matthews himself often shows a depth and thoughtfulness in interviews; a curiosity about, concern for, and understanding of the world often passed over by those disinterested in more than a surface-level judgment of his music.

An exploration of the spiritual themes we can find in this or any musician's art can help us do several things. First, it can inspire and encourage us to think about the band's lyrics in a new way, as

1. Meyer, "Phish, Dead & Company," para. 2.

well as consider our own beliefs in a different light. Second, it can help us gain a greater understanding of what the music originally intended to say, as well as how it nevertheless may be speaking into our own lives in a manner we weren't able to hear before. Third, it can give us a greater appreciation for music in general, and the ability of its combination of instrumental arrangement and lyrical thoughtfulness to engage our minds and emotions to communicate something powerful, even and especially if we may not have the words to describe how.

These three principles will underlie everything written in the forthcoming chapters.

LET'S BE HONEST ABOUT A FEW THINGS FIRST

Aside from the principles mentioned above, several other working assumptions will guide the content of this book.

First, how do I define "spirituality?" In its simplest terms, I mean our sense of connection to a transcendent, to others, and to ourselves.[2] Here's what I mean by each.

When I talk about a transcendent, the first thing many may think of is God. Those of us steeped in a culture that emphasizes or assumes Western definitions of God may immediately picture an image of a divine personage that is somehow above, around, or within us. For many, this concept provides a guiding point for how they think about a transcendent being that exists beyond us and that somehow grounds or moves all of existence.

But not everyone does so. Some Eastern religious traditions may conceptualize the transcendent as more of an impersonal force residing within us or in nature that we may grow closer to through prayer and other means. For still others, they may speak of the transcendent in terms of a Higher Power, the Universe, nature, or simply the Unknown. Matthews himself once shared that he often

---

2. For a more in-depth treatment of this definition, see my first book, *Coffeehouse Contemplative: Spiritual Direction for the Everyday* (Aurora, CO: Noesis, 2016).

uses the word "God" as shorthand for everything he doesn't know.[3] He may not be the only one. For him, as for many others, God is equivalent to mystery or what is beyond our knowledge, perhaps as a more impersonal force that guides things along, or as a passive presence whose actions are more beyond our comprehension.

Part of our spirituality is how we define this sense of otherness beyond us, as well as our relationship to it. Sometimes we actively nurture or explore that relationship, whether through study or meditation or worship, or some other regular discipline. Sometimes we may believe something about it while also remaining content not to pursue any exploration of the topic beyond that.

Even if he may define "God" as everything he doesn't know, Matthews does have ideas about what God is and isn't, and it mostly shows up in songs and interviews as critiques of the traditional ideas about God already mentioned. He often questions what happens when those ideas don't measure up to experience or produce tangible results. And even so, those critiques raise questions that people of faith may use to evaluate their own theological viewpoint. It is my belief, and it will be the approach of this book, that such critique can be edifying rather than cause for fear, resistance, or condemnation.

Another aspect of spirituality is how we conceptualize our relationships with others. At times this is informed by our sense of and relationship to a transcendent, and at other times it may be framed more by our relationship to ourselves, which I'll mention shortly. But this aspect of spirituality invites questions primarily about who we are relative to other people. Are we meant to serve or help them in some way? How often do we consider the effect that our actions have on others, or do we think it's not that important to think about? Do we value people in terms of their usefulness to us, or in terms of what we believe we can do for them? These sorts of questions guide our sense of spiritual relationship with others.

From his earliest experiences in South Africa to his later involvement in causes that he believes in, Matthews has a keen sense of how critical our relationships and sense of connection to others

---

3. Graham, "Rock Star Dave Matthews on God," para. 7.

are to the survival of our planet. His songs often focus on why it matters that we show love and concern for each other, because a sense of common purpose is what helps individuals, communities, and entire countries endure.

Finally, spirituality involves how we connect with ourselves. This includes self-awareness—what we are thinking and feeling at any moment, and why. This also includes self-identification—who we believe we are, and who we are becoming or meant to become. This includes our sense of place in the world, which involves how we think about our relationship to others and to a transcendent. Again, we may take on various forms of study and practice to nurture this awareness.

When I reference spirituality over the course of this book, I will be using these ways to guide my definition, and how I will approach Dave Matthews Band's music.

I must mention one other thing before we move on. My own spiritual tradition is Christian, specifically a strand of non-evangelical American Protestantism. This background will inevitably guide my explorations, and I will often draw from Christian spirituality in these reflections. My hope is that you come away with a greater understanding of spirituality in general, and if your background is not Christian or you left that tradition the first chance you had, I hope that you'll find something here that will inform your spirituality as you now understand it.

What I aim to do in this work is allow Dave Matthews Band's songs to provide the true starting point from which conversation flows. I will do my best to refrain from beginning with some other point that I want to make while hunting down the songs that will help bolster my case. To be honest, I've been a fan of this band for too long to see the latter approach as anything other than disrespectful to their art; I want to honor the source material as best I can. I'll probably make mistakes anyway, and I only have so much control over how readers will receive what I write, but that is what I strive to do.

That said, you may notice that there are no actual lyrics printed in this book. The process for asking permission to reprint them can come with a long wait and a steep cost. I attempt to describe what the songs are talking about without quoting them directly. As you encounter references to each song, you may want to pause and listen to it through whatever legal means are available to you before continuing.

WHAT ARE WE TALKING ABOUT?

With all that out of the way, here's where we'll go over the remainder of the book.

Chapter 2 will be a basic introduction to the members of Dave Matthews Band, as well as the ups and downs of their careers as a group. Before we delve into their music, we should spend a little time learning about where they've been.

Chapter 3 will explore the strong theme in Dave Matthews Band's songs that decry institutional forms of religion and belief. Such forms have at times proven to be quite destructive and betraying of their guiding principles. We'll consider what could be left behind in favor of a more dynamic and liberated form of faith and practice.

Chapter 4 will reflect on how Matthews talks and sings and thinks about God, whether it's everything he doesn't know, or some other way to think about a transcendent. This will include how God relates to or is involved with us, and we will think about spiritual traditions that reflect particularly on God's absence or our inability to define who or what God is.

Matthews occasionally sings specifically about Jesus. While he doesn't necessarily think much about the theological or metaphysical claims that Christians make about him, he seems to be an admirer of the man. Chapter 5 will explore why and how this is so, and what we still could learn from Jesus, even if we don't believe doctrinal statements about him.

In chapter 6, we'll look at the strong streak of encouragement in Dave Matthews Band's music to adopt a "seize the day" approach to life. As much as we may focus on where we've been or the possibilities of where we'd like to go, how important is our present moment, and how are we meant to think about it?

However, as often as Dave Matthews Band sings about making the most of life every day, they also seem to recognize that there is a balance to maintain between enjoyment and abuse. Chapter 7 will explore how, even though their music sometimes celebrates what life has to offer, they also sometimes caution against overindulgence and greed.

Chapter 8 will be an exploration of one's own identity. Several of Dave Matthews Band's songs question what would happen if we were someone other than we are, both in terms of the possibilities and the drawbacks. As mentioned, an important aspect of spirituality is how we connect to ourselves, and the band's music reflects on this more than once.

Just as important to connecting with ourselves is connecting to others. Dave Matthews Band's songs sometimes speak of the critical nature of thinking about our impact on others or how much more effective we'd be if we banded together around a common purpose. Chapter 9 will discuss this in depth.

In chapter 10, we will think about the potential fruits of such cooperation. Matthews sometimes sings of taking action beyond mere speech or belief, and the real difference such movement can make. We will see how spirituality inspires us to act.

The band has suffered tragedy both individually and as a group, perhaps most notably the loss of founding member LeRoi Moore in 2008. Chapter 11 will consider some of their songs about death and grief, as well as explore how, even in loss, there can be cause for hope.

My hope is that those less familiar with the band's catalogue will have a greater appreciation of these artists that have been entertaining and enriching fans for over twenty-five years. I also hope that those curious about faith may find some inroads to continue their own journey, or that this may help heal spiritual wounds by presenting an alternative to damaging beliefs to which you may have been subjected in the past. In the best of circumstances, I hope that you find at least a little of each.

2

A BRIEF BAND HISTORY

David J. Matthews was born in Johannesburg, South Africa on January 9, 1967 to John and Val Matthews. Just ten years prior, South Africa had become an independent nation, although many people within its borders were not truly free. This was the era of apartheid, where the white minority still held power over the black majority. The country was a police state, lording restrictions over much of the population and giving preferential treatment to a smaller ruling class, all determined by racial lines.

Matthews's experiences in his formative years left an impression for which he ultimately was glad, although it didn't come without painful moments. When Matthews was ten years old, John died of lung cancer. Val was a devoted Quaker and part of a faith-based anti-apartheid movement in South Africa. She impressed on Dave, as well as his siblings Jane, Anne, and Peter, the importance of recognizing and honoring differences in others rather than living as if they deserved special privileges. Interracial harmony and pacifism were central values instilled in the Matthews children beginning in their youngest years, and Dave took them to heart.[1]

After a few years in New York, the family moved back to South Africa, where Dave spent most of his teenage years until

1. Martell, *Music for the People*, 4.

it came close to time for his mandatory service in the country's military. At this point, Val moved the children back to the United States, eventually settling in Charlottesville, Virginia, when he was nineteen years old.[2]

Matthews also grew up with music, both the sacred songs he learned from Quaker tradition and the popular musicians he heard on the radio. As a teenager, he also developed an interest in playing guitar. A self-taught musician, he was drawn to the acoustic version of the instrument. Rather than learning to play through traditional lessons, he opted to approach the guitar as more of something on which to play percussion, learning chords and notes as he explored its potential as a string instrument doubling as a drum.[3]

Matthews began tinkering with songwriting, as well as seeking opportunities to play in front of people. The door he needed to open came in the form of getting a job as a bartender at popular Charlottesville venue Miller's, where he met David Roebuck, another musician who'd had some success in the 1980s with a band called The Deal. Roebuck helped Matthews finish and record his first song, "The Song That Jane Likes."[4]

As Matthews gained more confidence in his playing and songwriting, he approached other local musicians to collaborate with. This included guitarist Tim Reynolds, who would let Matthews sit in with his band TR3, and who has been one of his longest musical relationships. This also included drummer Carter Beauford and saxophonist LeRoi Moore, who were both older and more accomplished, but saw something in Matthews's playing style that made them agree to contribute to the demo recording that he wanted to put together.

Initial rehearsals with Matthews, Beauford, and Moore didn't go as smoothly as hoped, so the trio had the idea to add a fourth: a sixteen-year-old jazz bass student named Stefan Lessard.[5] Now

2. Delancey, *Step Into the Light*, 9–10.
3. Martell, *Music for the People*, 59.
4. Van Noy, *So Much to Say*, 17–18.
5. Martell, *Music for the People*, 15.

a foursome, the group began playing frat parties and at bars, becoming more comfortable with each other's playing the more they performed together.

As the band continued to lay down recordings, they decided that one track, "Tripping Billies," would benefit from including a violin. The group found Boyd Tinsley, who was playing with several area groups by that point, to contribute. After recording his part, he began guesting with them during live gigs as his schedule allowed, and eventually became a permanent fixture.[6]

After the lineup was finally set, the band continued to play in larger and larger venues. Naturally, they needed to identify themselves so that people knew where they were performing, and the name on which they settled was more accidental than intentional. Leading up to one gig, the group was pressed for a name to put on the flyer, and Tinsley just wrote, "Dave Matthews Band."[7] It didn't take long before the band's popularity wouldn't allow them to change it. Although the name suggests that the group is a frontman with a handful of backup musicians, the band has long insisted that their songwriting is much more collaborative in nature.

The officially-named Dave Matthews Band released their first album, *Remember Two Things*, on December 16, 1993. Many of the tracks are recordings from live performances, while several are live takes of Matthews and Reynolds playing acoustic duets. Some of the songs included on this first release would make appearances as refined studio versions on later albums. But at this point, with a set lineup, a name, and an album to promote, the band was beginning to find a wider audience.

THE BIG THREE

Longtime fans of Dave Matthews Band will tell you that, even though the group releases a studio album every few years, the true driver of their popularity and success has always been their live

---

6. Delancey, *Step Into the Light*, 48.
7. Martell, *Music for the People*, 20.

show. From their earliest years, the band has maintained a relentless tour schedule with the exceptions of two year-long breaks in 2011 and 2017. Even despite their stated intentions during these two hiatuses, they still performed several times as a full band, or just as a Matthews/Reynolds pairing.

The band's love of performing live has always been their lifeblood, which was how they developed their following in their earliest days. In addition to booking venues as often as they could, they also allowed people to bring recorders to tape their shows; even letting people plug their devices directly into the soundboard. Those who'd record could then make arrangements with other fans to send copies of shows far beyond the band's sphere of influence. Through an extensive network of word-of-mouth, tape trading, and early internet communities, the band's music traveled far beyond Charlottesville to surrounding states, across the country, and into Canada. As a result, people were able to hear the band in their element, complete with long jams and interplay between this unique collection of instruments and styles that would make each rendering of a song different than the last. In those earliest years, the band would be surprised to hear their music blaring from cars as they traveled to play in states to which they hadn't been before.[8]

While the band found some success in releasing *Remember Two Things*, it was their popularity that had resulted from relentless touring and encouragement of tape trading that led to RCA contacting them to work on their first complete studio album. They had road-tested so many songs by this point that going into the studio became an exercise in deciding which ones to focus on and craft into workable arrangements for the medium, rather than writing brand new material.

For this effort, the band chose producer Steve Lillywhite to helm the project. By the point Lillywhite began working with the band, he'd already amassed a long line of accomplishments, including work with XTC, Peter Gabriel, U2, and the Talking Heads.

Lillywhite made his intentions with the band clear from the beginning: he wouldn't set out to change their sound, he would

8. Delancey, *Step Into the Light*, 80–81.

instead just help them harness and control it enough for the purposes of an album.[9] He and the band developed a natural rapport, which would prove significant for later full albums and other recordings.

Under the Table and Dreaming was released on September 24, 1994, with its first single, "What Would You Say," receiving extensive airplay the following February. The band continued to tour to support the album, and its eclectic, uncategorizable sound had been introduced to an even larger audience. By May of 1995, the album was certified platinum and peaked on Billboard at the eleventh spot a month later.[10] Subsequent singles such as "Ants Marching" and "Satellite" were released not long after.

This surge in success led to another discovery by new fans: they weren't guaranteed to hear the radio singles at every show. Keeping in the spirit of their pre-*Under the Table and Dreaming* days, they wanted to make each setlist its own experience, and they even made a conscious effort to leave "What Would You Say" off the card for much of their touring immediately after the album's release, not wanting to depend on it for a crowd's reaction.[11] The band has continued this practice to this day, where concertgoers are seldom guaranteed to hear many familiar hits.

After performing in support of their first major label release, the band re-entered the studio to work on their second. Once again, they already had a deep catalogue of songs to hone into workable album tunes, and Steve Lillywhite returned for this new effort. The band decided that, rather than try to recreate anything that they did on *Under the Table and Dreaming*, they'd come at this new album with a clean slate to see what developed. This ended up involving less of recording the parts individually or using click tracks in favor of the entire band playing in a circle live.[12]

The result, *Crash*, was released on April 30, 1996. It debuted in the second spot on Billboard and the first single, "Too Much,"

9. Martell, *Music for the People*, 35.
10. Martell, *Music for the People*, 47.
11. Martell, *Music for the People*, 45.
12. Delancey, *Step Into the Light*, 171.

received extensive play on radio; the video was also prominent on MTV. Follow-up singles from *Crash* included perhaps one of their most popular songs, "Crash Into Me," the studio version of "Tripping Billies," and "So Much To Say." "So Much To Say" also was nominated for a Grammy award for Best Rock Performance by a Duo or Group in 1997, which the band won.

Now enjoying a steady stream of success and recognition through album and single rankings, constant touring, and receiving awards, it was again time to enter the studio. Steve Lillywhite joined the band for a third time, but they decided not to rely so much on songs from the road. Having begun work in a California studio in the fall of 1997, they experimented with new sounds, arrangements, instruments, and guest musicians. Along with Tim Reynolds, who also appeared on their previous two albums, the Kronos Quartet provided strings for several songs, and Alanis Morissette sang on two songs for the album as well.

Before These Crowded Streets released on April 28, 1998, debuting at number one on Billboard. While retaining some of the band's signature style, this album's combination of guest artists, a richer sound, and multiple unlisted interludes connecting the songs signaled a depth that hadn't appeared on their previous releases. Critics compared it to other artists' most successful and adventurous outings such as The Police's *Synchronicity* and U2's *The Joshua Tree* as a way of announcing that the band had reached a new level of musical accomplishment.[13]

This trio of albums is often called "The Big Three" by diehard fans due to what they see as a special mix of the band's energy, unique sound, and live creativity harnessed for studio sessions. For some, this term is used as a way of longing for something they believe the band hasn't achieved on their albums since. For others, it is simply a shorthand reference to the vintage collection of songs that began their fandom.

After "The Big Three" and almost a decade of enjoying an uphill climb, the band was about to hit some rocky terrain.

---

13. Delancey, *Step Into the Light*, 222.

TROUBLED TIMES AND NEW SOUNDS

In the winter of 2000, having enjoyed the benefits of three well-received albums in a row as well as a robust touring schedule, the band re-entered the recording studio with Steve Lillywhite. For these sessions, they purchased a studio in their hometown of Charlottesville called Haunted Hollow, thinking they'd benefit from recording near where they lived. In retrospect, they decided that this space did not meet their needs at the time, but they persisted without realizing the effect it—along with other unspoken issues—was having on their efforts.[14]

Thanks to the rise in technology and of sharing information on the internet, more news was available about these sessions than with previous efforts. People would share clips of new songs online, as well as post other news and rumors about the sessions as they heard them. Among other things, two pieces of information or hearsay stood out as the band strove to make this latest album. First was the sense that these songs seemed to be some of the darkest they'd ever written, both in terms of lyrical content and musical tone. Second was rumblings that the band was experiencing dissension while cooped up together in Haunted Hollow.[15]

Eventually, the record company announced that the release date for this album would be pushed back as the band struggled to finish the songs. In the meantime, they went out on tour yet again, even including songs they were working on in their setlists. As they continued to try to complete their work on the album, an executive from RCA, David Flohr, flew out to hear the new material, and his reaction was similar to most fans': the songs were dark and depressing.

Flohr pulled the band aside without Matthews to ask if they were feeling the same way he was about the music, and they agreed: it wasn't working. They confronted Dave himself about how they felt, and he was able to hear their concerns, even admitting that he'd been in a dark and creatively stifling place. Their chosen

14. Van Noy, *So Much to Say*, 98.
15. Van Noy, *So Much to Say*, 100.

solution was twofold: get out of Haunted Hollow, and part ways with Lillywhite to see if working with a different producer would reignite their inspiration.[16]

Matthews flew to California by himself to meet with Glen Ballard, a producer known for his pop and rock background. One of his most notable claims to fame at that point was his work with Alanis Morissette on her debut album *Jagged Little Pill*, but he'd also worked with No Doubt and Aerosmith, among others.

The chemistry between Matthews and Ballard was instantaneous. Matthews describes sitting down and immediately feeling inspired, to the point of writing nine new songs in ten days.[17] However, these new pieces were far different from anything he or the band had written before. First, Matthews elected to use an electric guitar as his primary instrument rather than his usual acoustic. Second, the songs were much shorter than the extended jam-infested works the group was known for. Third, when the band eventually joined Matthews out west, they were handed sheet music rather than invited to flesh out the songs with their own ideas.[18]

Everyday was released on February 27, 2001. It featured tight rock arrangements that were friendlier to and more ready for pop radio than anything they'd done before. While it sold well, many old fans didn't know what to make of what sounded like such a radical departure from what they were used to. In addition to the prominence of Matthews's electric guitar playing, Moore's saxophone was diminished and Tinsley's violin was almost non-existent. To many, this Dave Matthews Band album didn't sound much like Dave Matthews Band at all.

About a month later, something happened that the band didn't anticipate. While fans were still trying to make sense of *Everyday*, the unreleased tracks they'd recorded with Lillywhite were released on the internet. Dubbed *The Lillywhite Sessions*, this unofficial "album" was downloaded over five thousand times the first day it appeared, and within a few years would surpass a million.

16. Delancey, *Step Into the Light*, 240–42.
17. Martell, *Music for the People*, 140.
18. Martell, *Music for the People*, 141–42.

Between *Everyday* and these recordings, fans suddenly had an embarrassment of riches, with many expressing a preference for the abandoned songs over and against the official album.

The release of *The Lillywhite Sessions* helped inspire the band to get back to the studio to take care of unfinished business. Returning to where they'd recorded *Before These Crowded Streets*, they polished up nine of the unreleased songs and added two new ones, one of which—"Where Are You Going"—was featured in the Adam Sandler movie *Mr. Deeds*.

The result, *Busted Stuff*, was released on July 16, 2002. Even though it consisted of many of the *Lillywhite Sessions* songs, there was a difference in tone between the previous darker versions and these new official ones. Matthews would express his own preference for the new studio recordings, believing that they were able to give the songs the treatment they needed, including adding a certain lightness to them that he believed was missing from the earlier renditions.[19] Even so, critics and fans continue to compare the two sets of recordings, with many preferring the more brooding versions on the *Sessions*. The debate rages on.

By this point in the band's life, individual members became more interested in pursuing personal projects in addition to what they did as a group. In 2003, Matthews released his first solo album, *Some Devil*, and toured with a separate group of musicians that included Reynolds and Phish guitarist Trey Anastasio. Tinsley also released his own album, *True Reflections*, the title track of which the band had performed on occasion during concerts. Everyone was quick to assure fans that this didn't mean the band was ending, but also expressed that being able to work on other things helped them renew their creativity and passion for what they did together.[20]

The band reconvened in early 2005 to record their next album, this time with producer Mark Batson, who was most known for his work with rap and R&B artists. They also returned to an improved and expanded Haunted Hollow for this work. The result,

19. Chonin, "In the Studio," para. 5.
20. Martell, *Music for the People*, 160.

Stand Up, released on May 10, 2005. As with *Everyday*, fans expressed disappointment that it once again didn't mark a full return to their Big Three sound. It was again absent of any jam sessions and featured elements of Batson's influence with some electronic elements and strong backbeats. Many began to wonder if they'd ever get something out of the band reminiscent of their early music again.

TRAGEDY AND REBIRTH

While the band has brought many guests onstage during their live performances over the years, they made a significant shift in the summer of 2006 by including trumpeter Rashawn Ross as part of their lineup. Dubbed a "touring member," Ross's presence was to complement Moore's saxophone playing, to create a true horn section. This signaled a shift in musical philosophy, where even though horns had not been as prominent on recent albums, they at least would be during their shows.[21]

In 2007, the band headed back into the studio with Batson to work on another album, although general mainstream news and enthusiasm about the possibility of a new release had been tempered by shifts in the industry and general reception of *Stand Up*. In early 2008, the band announced that they'd chosen Rob Cavallo to helm their latest recording efforts, which received a warmer reception as a natural fit for the band than Ballard or Batson had been.[22] In addition, Tim Reynolds joined the band as another "touring member" for their full 2008 summer tour, which was another welcome move for fans.

Things seemed to be looking up, but nothing could have prepared the band for what happened later that summer.

On June 30, LeRoi Moore spent a rare day off at his home, as did other band members due to the tour's stops being so close to where they lived. Moore took his ATV out for a ride around his

---

21. Van Noy, *So Much to Say*, 141.

22. Van Noy, *So Much to Say*, 147.

property, but couldn't see a ditch in front of him that caused his vehicle to flip over. He was transported to the University of Virginia hospital, and the band quickly released a statement that he wouldn't continue on their tour so he could recover from his injuries. Jeff Coffin, the saxophonist for Bela Fleck and the Flecktones and a familiar friend of the band, stood in for Moore for the rest of their summer dates as he could.[23] The band did their best to keep their own heads up, as well as support Moore and offer updates on his recovery during concerts.

On August 19, 2008, rumors began circulating that Moore had succumbed to his injuries and passed away. The band addressed this in two ways: first, by posting a simple graphic of Moore on their website's front page; and second, by insisting that they still walk onstage for their scheduled concert that evening in Los Angeles, during which Matthews stepped to the microphone and confirmed what everyone feared. Despite this news of tragedy that most would expect would hang over the evening like a dark cloud, the band made it a point to pour their energy into that evening's performance as a tribute to their friend.[24]

While many expected the band to take time off or cancel the rest of that year's shows, they insisted on continuing in Moore's memory. They also had a new resolve to finish the album they'd been working on, making it a special point to dedicate it to their lost bandmate. Part of that motivation was Moore's vision for what their next album should be. Matthews has shared that Moore kept insisting that their studio albums should be as rich and deep and exciting as their live shows, and with this sentiment still ringing in the band's ears, they set to work to honor his vision.[25]

By this point, the band had various jams, improvisations, and licks that Moore had already recorded that they made a point to incorporate into their recording. While Coffin would flesh out songs as needed, they tried to put as much of what they had from Moore into these latest tracks as they could. This would be immediately

23. Van Noy, *So Much to Say*, 153.
24. Wener, "Dave Matthews Band's Farewell," para. 4, 6.
25. Welch, "Interview With a Jampire," para. 9.

evident on the first track, "Grux," which is Moore playing a soulful riff by himself.

Big Whiskey & the GrooGrux King was released on June 2, 2009. "Grux" was a nickname the other members had for Moore, and its incorporation into the title was another signal that this album was for him. This translated to their live shows as well, with the band carrying memories and intentions to attribute every night to him inspiring their performances.[26]

In 2009 and the years that followed, Ross, Coffin, and Reynolds became permanent fixtures of the band, first evidenced by their inclusion on *Big Whiskey* and their annual tour dates. When the band returned to the studio to work on another album, it had become clear that the trio was with the band to stay.

After electing to take 2011 off from touring as a unit, the band returned in force the next year for a full slate of live dates. These shows featured new songs from *Away From the World*, which was released on September 11, 2012. As with *Big Whiskey*, this album showed more of a return to the sound of their Big Three albums, with Tinsley's violin in particular the most prominent it had been since *Busted Stuff*. It wasn't a full reversion to those earlier efforts, but a complete evolution into what the band had become due both to tragedy and the incorporation of new players.

After several more years of full tour slates, the band again took 2017 off, leaving many fans wondering what this signaled for their future. They had a strong answer in early 2018, announcing an extensive list of performances all around the country, as well as a new album to be released in the summer. They were ready to get back to work in a big way, and its millions of fans received this news with excitement.

As with any band that has been around as long as they have, Dave Matthews Band continues to chart new territory for itself. Now that we've considered where they've been, we can take a closer look at some of the ideas that their music has expressed along the way.

---

26. Kelly, "Stefan Lessard," para. 26.

3

FAITH'S POTENTIAL FOR HARM AND GOOD

Years ago, I had a friend who had frequent clashes with a group of evangelical Christians that she was involved with. She had a background in Wiccan belief and practice, but also had begun exploring various aspects of Christian faith and was striving to reconcile these systems as she understood each of them. These attempts at meshing the two did not sit well with this pocket of believers, and their reactions to her often crossed the line from intellectual to personal.

One day, this friend came to me wanting to talk about some problems she was having in her relationship with her boyfriend. I listened to her for a while, trying to formulate a response that would lend support or reassurance. Finally, I came up with a verse from the book of Jeremiah that I thought would be helpful to her, and as I began to quote it she stopped me and said, "I just want you to know that you are one of the only people I'll still let quote the Bible to me."

This exchange sticks with me because it was so unique but also because the experience it speaks to is so common. By that point she'd had enough negative interactions with other Christians that she'd become weary and wary of the entire enterprise, including Bible verses quoted at her by antagonistic people. She'd come to a point where she'd lost patience with the majority of those using the Bible at all due to how they used it with her: to attack, demean, and insult. Some may have claimed they were doing so out of love, but she'd experienced nothing loving about their actions.

This experience, as I said, has become quite common. In the United States, the percentage of people that considers itself "unaffiliated" with any form of organized religion is on the rise, with 66 percent of those who consider themselves part of that group thinking that organized religion has a negative effect on society rather than a positive one.[1]

What causes such a view? A variety of things. Like my friend in my story, it could be a series of negative interactions with people who claim a certain religion. It could involve seeing groups who profess certain religion-based beliefs on the news expressing themselves in belligerent ways. It could be the way religious groups intertwine themselves with political parties, striving for power and control rather than kindness and service. It could be an inability to reconcile certain beliefs or doctrines with personal experience or scientific findings, and believers' unwillingness to engage one's questions or doubts.

In a 2009 interview, Dave Matthews told part of his own story that led him to question and eventually reject formal systems of belief. This included his realization that the existence of hell would mean that many good people he admired, including his father, would end up there.[2] This reflects a somewhat common objection to such a belief: once one realizes that people like Anne Frank, Gandhi, and a generous, giving atheist neighbor would be consigned to eternal torment, they begin to question whether hell exists, but also what kind of a God would do such a thing.

1. Cooper et al., "Exodus," para. 23.
2. Q on CBC, "Dave Matthews," 32:24–33:41.

As I've mentioned, this is an increasingly common occurrence. While many still may see the usefulness of organized religion for instilling morals and helping others, a growing number does not. Can anything be done about this? What use, if any, might faith still have for people despite such a negative perception?

FORMS OF FAITH: CREED AND TRUST

The song "Eh Hee" is a single that Matthews released on September 4, 2007. He played all the instruments for it, and an accompanying video was released the same day. One of the refrains is a chant based in the music of the San tribe of South Africa, which inspired Matthews to write the song.[3]

After the opening chant, the first words in English seem to be an acknowledgement of the various religious traditions found all over the world, and the different ways they name and conceptualize God. However, there are also many ways that we either name or carry out evil, big and small, some of which we own ourselves but much more that we blame on other people or entities. These opening lines are not a judgment on religious practice or belief; rather, they are a reminder of the diversity of belief that people hold.

While this song does not seem to take issue with belief in general, it does zero in on certain forms that insist on their own interpretation of the world as absolute. Such a tight holding of belief without nuance, without allowing new experience or information to allow one's view to evolve and change, can lead to stunted personal growth, as well as become hurtful to others. And as the study cited earlier indicates, belief in a world with very clear delineations of right and wrong by some religious communities is becoming less and less convincing to many due to the wealth of knowledge we have at our fingertips.

"Eh Hee" describes a person disoriented by reality. There's so much going on that he finds it difficult to make sense of it or to keep up. At times, he can approach it with humor, but even then

---

3. "Eh Hee," lines 13–20.

it takes a great deal of willpower to walk or to crawl forward; to carry on despite the massive amount of uncertainty around him. Holding onto a faith that things can improve or that we can rely on forms of support and guidance both seen and unseen can be difficult when such confusion seems so ever-present and disruptive.

People work with several definitions of the word "faith," two of which we'll briefly discuss. The first definition equates it to a set of beliefs one assents to intellectually. A synonym for this concept of faith might be "creed." That is, we may talk about "what my faith tells me" about God, humanity, prayer, how to live, and so on. This definition of faith is the kind that "Eh Hee" cautions against, because it can veer into destructive behavior by its adherents if gripped too tightly.

We come to our own faith-as-creed in different ways. We may base it on what we were taught at a young age, which may or may not have evolved as we've grown older (and this itself may have multiple causes behind it). We may hold to a certain faith-as-creed less because we're personally invested in it, and more to continue enjoying acceptance with certain social circles or to avoid family conflict. Or our faith-as-creed might be more dynamic and changing, informed by new experiences and helping us grow and understand the world, while we are also trying to understand what we believe ourselves.

A second possible way to think about faith is in terms of trust. This type goes beyond what one believes, translating that belief into action. We may encounter quite a bit of confusion over the course of our day, between responsibilities to work or family; problems related to relationships, health, or finances; or keeping up with what is happening in our community, country, or world. Taking even one further step forward, trusting that things can be better and that one can face the problems and opportunities ahead, can require a lot of energy. Even when parts of our faith-as-creed waver or have seemed to fail, our faith-as-trust may help us to endure.

Returning to my conversation with my friend, she was seeking cause for faith-as-trust, to keep going despite the uncertainty and despair she was facing. Meanwhile, she'd received too much faith-as-creed (including from me) as one after another had attempted to shoehorn her beliefs and experiences into a certain view of the world; even using bullying tactics to do it. And this approach had ended up compounding the problem rather than addressing it in any meaningful or constructive way.

Faith-as-trust helps us take steps forward. Mind you, faith-as-creed also has the power to do this. It has the capacity to remind us of many beautiful things about life, about hope, about how to strive for peace and how to love others, about our own belovedness as people and connection to the rest of an equally beloved creation. Faith-as-creed can provide grounding and spiritual nourishment. But our days may bring events that faith-as-creed couldn't have accounted for on its own, and those times bring questions as to how we may reconcile or apply our faith-as-creed with what has happened. We may ask how it still brings us hope and grounding, or whether something about our faith-as-creed needs to shift in response.

Faith-as-creed certainly can be life-giving, if one allows it to move and change and react as we do. And it often takes faith-as-trust for that to happen.

WHEN FAITH TURNS DEADLY

"The Last Stop" is the third track on the band's 1998 release *Before These Crowded Streets*. The main riff, led by Moore's saxophone and Tinsley's violin, has an Eastern sound that powers the song. Matthews himself has described his appreciation for Eastern forms of music due to how much it lends itself to improvisation and a sense of chaos, which to him help give it a unique and even sacred quality.[4]

If the music of "The Last Stop" has a frantic, driving tone, the lyrics match it in intensity. In the same interview where he expresses his admiration for Eastern music, he states that the song

4. Vogel, "Finding The Groove," para. 16.

stemmed from a frustration with how people give unwavering and unquestioning adherence to national leadership, no matter their destructive intentions or the harmful results their actions produce. Life is more complex and multilayered than that, and one cannot give absolute loyalty or ascribe absolute goodness to people or ideas, especially if outcomes are clear that they restrict or destroy life rather than expand or enhance it.[5]

From the opening verse, which is vivid and jarring, Matthews decries engaging in hatred and killing of others without questioning why or whether it is wrong. It paints a picture of a sky lit by the fires of destruction, either from that which is still raging or its aftermath, the result of violence led by blind ideology. The world in this song is a smoldering mess, the piles of victims visible in the mind's eye as Matthews describes the resulting damage of what humanity puts one another through.

The cause of such violence could be political conflict between nations, as Matthews characterizes it. However, this song includes religious allusions as well. He makes several clear references to Jesus being nailed on a cross, although the way he uses it is not in a positive or redemptive way. Rather, he includes it to point out how some may use this belief to justify their conduct toward others. If one believes their actions—right or wrong—are nonetheless covered by God's saving or forgiving action through Jesus' death, one might believe they are able to do whatever they wish. This may be compounded by the belief that one's own religious viewpoint is correct over and against anyone else's.

"The Last Stop" is a hard pushback against the most egregious and extreme and largest-scale downsides of faith-as-creed. History is filled with examples of groups of people believing that they are God's chosen nation, race, or religion, and are thus justified in their violent and oppressive actions toward others, covered by God's favor or forgiveness. This includes movements when faith-as-creed has been used in cynical ways to sway public support for conduct that looks little like what God might really want, but due

---

5. Vogel, "Finding The Groove," paras. 17–19.

to blind faith—as Matthews says—people go along with it because the right words were used by one's leaders to rationalize it.

Many passages in the Bible call not only individuals, but nations, to account for the ways they treat the poorest and most vulnerable among them. Many of the prophets in the Old Testament do so, as they understood their calling to be to proclaim God's message to the kingdoms of Israel and Judah. One of the best examples comes from a smaller book named after the prophet Amos:

> Therefore thus says the Lord, the God of hosts, the Lord: In all the squares there shall be wailing; and in all the streets they shall say, "Alas! alas!" They shall call the farmers to mourning, and those skilled in lamentation, to wailing; [17]in all the vineyards there shall be wailing, for I will pass through the midst of you, says the Lord. [18]Alas for you who desire the day of the Lord! Why do you want the day of the Lord? It is darkness, not light; [19]as if someone fled from a lion, and was met by a bear; or went into the house and rested a hand against the wall, and was bitten by a snake. [20]Is not the day of the Lord darkness, not light, and gloom with no brightness in it? (Amos 5:16–20)

Here the people of Israel seem to have become smug and comfortable in their belief that they are God's chosen people. They are eagerly anticipating some future "day of the Lord," which they believe will be a great and glorious event where blessing will rain down and they will enjoy the full extent of God's favor and approval. When that day comes, they tell themselves, they will be able to bask in being divinely chosen in a new and wonderful existence.

But Amos paints a very different picture, one meant to burst the people's overconfident bubble: he says the people aren't going to like what's coming. The "day of the Lord" won't be enjoyable for them; rather, it will bring darkness and wailing. It will bring gloom and regret and despair. They have believed themselves to be righteous and ever-covered by God's forgiveness, but their conduct has instead brought God's anger and disapproval.

Amos continues:

I hate, I despise your festivals, and I take no delight in your solemn assemblies. ²²Even though you offer me your burnt offerings and grain offerings, I will not accept them; and the offerings of well-being of your fatted animals I will not look upon. ²³Take away from me the noise of your songs; I will not listen to the melody of your harps. ²⁴But let justice roll down like waters, and righteousness like an everflowing stream. ²⁵Did you bring to me sacrifices and offerings the forty years in the wilderness, O house of Israel? ²⁶You shall take up Sakkuth your king, and Kaiwan your star-god, your images, which you made for yourselves; ²⁷therefore I will take you into exile beyond Damascus, says the Lord, whose name is the God of hosts. (Amos 5:21–27)

Here Amos calls the people back to what God would like: justice and righteousness in the form of how they treat one another. They can't simply present the correct sacrifices and offerings; they won't be able to show up, pay the proper faith-as-creed lip service through songs and prayers, and expect to have their actions and attitudes covered no matter what. That form of belief alone isn't enough, and won't save them.

Amos's message is that one can't profess belief without action. One can't say they love God and then neglect those in greatest need. One can't rely on faith-as-creed if it has no follow-through grounded in humility, kindness, and fair treatment for all regardless of their own life status. God can see through that, and declares it insufficient.

Passages like these warn against the same blind self-pardoning that "The Last Stop" describes. Faith-as-creed must translate to loving and merciful action toward others.

For faith to be life-giving, it must feature freedom rather than constriction, affirmation rather than destruction. Certain approaches to faith-as-creed often present religious devotion as featuring judgment, punishment, and fear. My friend mentioned at the start of this chapter had experienced this approach, and was close to leaving it behind. And on the grandest scale, faith-as-creed can lead to war, discrimination, or justifying privilege at the expense of whatever group will not or cannot benefit, whether based on income, race, orientation, ability, or identity.

But as I have mentioned, faith-as-creed also has the potential for wonder and beauty. It may describe the ways God has created and is creating, how God loves people of all backgrounds through their struggles and despite their mistakes. Faith-as-creed may often present a view of the world that is infused with divine gifts of peace, joy, and reconciliation. When faith is used to call attention to the gifts that each day presents, it can be liberating rather than spiritually stifling.

To approach faith-as-creed in this way is often to incorporate faith-as-trust as well. It involves a certain level of imagination and awe; an acceptance of the diversity and strangeness inherent in our world. It approaches differences as gifts to be received and lessons to be learned rather than obstacles to overcome, challenges to subdue, or disobediences to snuff out.

Revisiting our ideas of faith-as-creed and faith-as-trust often carries benefits to our own well-being as well as that of others. Not only does it reshape how we treat and care for those who differ from us or who need resources or reassurance, but it also heals our own souls that may be closed off, hesitant, suspicious, or prejudiced. Taking the leap that faith-as-trust calls for opens us to new possibilities for our own lives and for our experience of the transcendent that we wouldn't notice or realize we needed otherwise. And such experience may often come from places and people we wouldn't expect. In turn, our faith-as-creed may be enriched, refined, and deepened. Moving from blindness to having our heart's eyes wide open shows us a truth we wouldn't have thought possible without first taking the risk.

4

WHAT GOD IS
(OR ISN'T) UP TO

No Dave Matthews Band song comes close to offering a complete idea or image of who God is or what God is like. If we delved into the personal beliefs of each member of the band's lineup, we will get eight unique answers as to the nature, character, and existence of some kind of divine or transcendent force or being, as well as why they do or do not believe certain things.

As the primary lyric writer, Matthews's beliefs tend to be most front and center, and he does reference God many times, though often in a single line. If one combs through the band's catalogue in search of a comprehensive picture of God, the result will be incomplete, to say the least.

When Matthews speaks about God or faith in interviews, he tends to dismiss a view of God that gives unique regard to everyone on earth. Many religious traditions hold such an image of God, and thus it tends to be more pervasive and common even in secular understandings or portrayals. But Matthews has said that this image is too beyond logic for his own ability to accept it. If God exists, he has said, he'd be willing to believe in a God that demands that we take care of each other rather than one who tears us down or gives us an excuse to watch the world burn because something better is coming after it ends.[1]

With these sorts of sentiments, Matthews is rejecting a specific view of God that he sees as small, capricious, and unnecessarily cruel. Furthermore, he rejects a view of God that is all-controlling, determining the course of existence outside of the influence of our own actions, because it lets people off the hook from extending kindness or questioning the cause of disaster or tragedy, among other potential problems.

Matthews's alternative suggestion for a God that demands care and responsibility is one that many would argue is presented by the prophets of the Jewish Scriptures (what Christians commonly call the Old Testament) and by Jesus. Both frequently call people to account for their own wrongdoing and to reorient their lives away from their selfish desires and ambitions that hurt others, or to serve people and look after their needs rather than worry only about oneself. In both cases, the people being called out in this way use God or religious tradition as their excuse for not caring for other people, and in some cases for seeking to do harm to them. We saw this in the Amos passage explored in the previous chapter; Jesus will be discussed in more depth later.

For the purposes of this chapter, however, Matthews is saying that if we are meant to believe in a certain correct concept of God as presented by a particular tradition, then he rejects it because he believes humanity is meant to do better. And if this image is the definitive one, and we somehow lose it or it becomes obsolete, what are we left with? When any working definition that we have of God begins to crumble, what do we do?

FAITH IN HYPOTHETICAL

The band's 2009 album *Big Whiskey & the GrooGrux King* includes a song called "Time Bomb." Opening with a soft and meandering

---

1. Q on CBC, "Dave Matthews," 31:00–32:10.

interaction between saxophone and guitar, Matthews eventually begins singing a series of "what if" questions over the top of the music as it builds behind him. Early in the song, for instance, he asks what would happen if aliens visited Earth. He seems to think it would have an impact on several aspects of our life together.

First, he wonders how people's idea of God would change if definitive proof came that we aren't the only planet inhabited by intelligent life. If our worldview is informed by a theology that assumes God made this world and all that is in it as a unique occurrence in all that we know and don't know about the vastness of the universe, how would such an arrival affect that?

Second, he asks what this might do for human conflict, some of which is inspired or justified by religious belief. If two nations are divided against each other due to disputes over ideology or geography or access to resources, would a visit by another planet's species replace that conflict with a newfound unity? And would such unity be based on a common curiosity or enmity; a sense that they need to explore a new relationship or combat a perceived threat together rather than continue in their former hostilities?

In an interview, Matthews once offered his own explanation of the song, where he outright states that it involves the death of God. He wonders what such a thing would do to people and what it would change for those who profess faith. What might happen, he wonders, if suddenly our sense of the universe became that much bigger?[2]

For Matthews, and perhaps for many others, such an appearance by extraterrestrial life would make a definitive case that God doesn't exist. The logic behind this stance is that so many belief traditions assume that we are somehow the center of all life, and that Earth is the peak action of a creative being. If life from elsewhere shows up, a lot of that might fall apart, or at least present serious challenges that one never had to consider before, beyond hypothetical questions or scenarios presented by popular culture.

The deeper question beyond this single alien example is this: what happens to belief when it is challenged by unmistakable evidence that some part of it is wrong or incomplete? Where some may find it possible to re-evaluate and adjust based on new information, others may find it easier or the natural conclusion to move away from one set of beliefs entirely.

Beyond the intellectual questions of such possibilities is the emotional impact. As "Time Bomb" continues to build, by the final chorus Matthews is yelling the lyrics more than singing them. The intended effect is one of desperation or sadness or frustration. Something of belief has fallen apart, and now the singer needs assistance figuring out what to do with the remnants. Maybe they can be reworked or fitted together differently, or maybe it's time to give up even if the person wishes he or she could continue seeing things in certain ways. And maybe on a long enough timeline, things will work out at least close to how one hopes.

In the meantime, what do we do? How do we cope? What happens if our view of God is challenged in some way? Does it fall apart, or does it present the possibility for something new?

DEALING WITH DARK NIGHTS

Saint John of the Cross was a Carmelite monk who lived in the 1500s in Spain. He became an influential teacher and practitioner of contemplative spirituality in that part of the world, having worked with and learned under another notable figure, Teresa of Avila.

One of his best-known written works is a short series of poems and reflections collectively called *The Dark Night of the Soul*, where he describes a process of growing closer to God only after a time of God feeling distant and one losing faith in many of the former practices, words, writings, and sentiments which used to bring comfort and inner peace. Whereas before such things provided the reassurance that one needed to endure in faith and comfort, they now only bring further heartbreak and bitterness.[3] When one is going through such a time, these observances only seem to

---

3. Saint John of the Cross, *Dark Night of the Soul*, 25.

compound the problem by serving as reminders of their former function, now painful amplifiers of God's perceived absence.

Any number of events or causes may set one down a path toward a "dark night," but Saint John of the Cross describes in some detail the features and general process that such an experience includes. First, not only does the person no longer find comfort in any God-related activities such as prayer, worship, or devotion, but they end up not finding comfort in much of anything. They become so disoriented and disillusioned that nothing one may experience through the senses will bring true, lasting relief.[4]

Second, the person going through a "dark night" will at the same time be fixated on memories of the comfort they used to have, and wonder if they no longer "deserve God" in some way. The soul is in such watchfulness for any sign of God's presence, while at the same time having misplaced feelings that God no longer wants to be with the person. Saint John is quick to add that this watchfulness is good because it is a sign of a deeper spiritual passion and vitality.[5]

Finally, the person experiencing a "dark night" will eventually realize that God can be experienced beyond good feelings, sensory experience, and intellectual satisfaction. Rather, the person will come to a new inner place where they derive comfort from a deeper knowing of God's presence with them that doesn't rely on a sense of ease that one may not be able to maintain from one moment to the next.[6] Put in the terms of the previous chapter, one's faith-as-creed may go through a reassessment, and one's faith-as-trust will enjoy a strengthening of reliance that will serve as a more robust foundation going forward.

In Saint John's view, this "dark night" eventually resolves. As a complete process of growth and enriched awareness of God, he sees such an experience as having lasting benefits for the person undergoing its discomfort and struggle. But we also must assume that many may not wish to see this through to the desired end as

4. Saint John of the Cross, *Dark Night of the Soul*, 27.
5. Saint John of the Cross, *Dark Night of the Soul*, 27.
6. Saint John of the Cross, *Dark Night of the Soul*, 29.

Saint John describes it, and many have not. Many could tell their own stories of God seeming increasingly distant, the usual avenues of access or connection seeming more superficial, until one day they concluded that God either doesn't care or doesn't exist. This is the same conclusion echoed by Matthews in interviews, where the concept of a God concerned with each individual's life seems more and more absurd because it doesn't seem to be playing out that way.

This is not to say that, based on experience, one or the other is right or wrong. Many have tried to face their own "dark night," and the wait and struggle seemed to go so long without any semblance of a resolution on the horizon, a deeper awareness of God beyond the senses never materializing. And many others could tell powerful stories of coming out on the other side stronger, their faith reinforced, their resolve to live according to a renewed sense of God's presence in their lives reaffirmed.

To deny the person whose dark night never resolved their experience, or to accuse them of doing something wrong, or to question their sense of commitment, is to pile on further shame, guilt, anger, or despair. Such a person likely already put themselves through all of that when going through their time of spiritual loss. Every journey is different, and while one's story of eventual resolution may be helpful and reassuring to some, it may also invite questions of why such a thing wasn't possible for another.

DARK AND GREY

"Grey Street" was the third and final single off the band's 2002 album *Busted Stuff*. It tells the story of a young woman feeling hopeless about her life and wishing to break out of whatever she thinks is keeping her where she is. Throughout the song, we hear about her dreaming of a different path for herself and trying to think of ways to change her situation. She has a yearning to walk away from everything that she knows so she can pursue something that won't leave her feeling so lonely and sad. At one point, someone even stands on her doorstep encouraging her to follow what she really wants to do. Her reaction is to call for help rather than follow through on this echoing of her own desires, which gives the hint that her situation is at least partially self-imposed.

But the song's subject also might be paralyzed by despair; so worn down by disappointment or anxiety that she can't conceive of a way out without imagining how it could all go wrong. Her need to muster a certain level of courage or hope or confidence seems to be her first concern. And so, among other things, she tries reaching out to God, even though she expresses doubt that God is really listening or will do anything.

This part of the song reflects Matthews's own sentiments from his interviews about how God, if God exists, interacts with the world. Just as he doesn't think there's such a thing as a God who personally cares for or directs the emotions and actions of every individual person, the protagonist of "Grey Street" seems to be experiencing this in her own life. According to this verse, she maintains a regular prayer practice (which could be little more than a nightly lament), believing that being so consistent in reaching out to God will help deliver her from her plight. However, she has never seen any kind of results, and this causes her to question whether she should move on to other tactics.

And yet for some reason, she remains hopeful. As emotionally and spiritually exhausted as she feels, she maintains some semblance of optimism that sharing her thoughts with God and asking God to provide some way out or forward will make a difference. But her question about the effectiveness of prayer, of faith, of God in general, remains.

The main character of "Grey Street" could be any of us; she is a representation of so many people on any given day. Her situation and simultaneous trust in and wariness of God's ability to help raise both common and serious questions about where God is or what God is doing. Even if we call it different things or our own struggles don't exactly line up with what Saint John of the Cross describes, the experience of a "dark night of the soul" leaves us often having the same sorts of wonderings as in the song: even if we have hope that one day God will show us something or take action or send us somebody, we also might wonder if we'd be better off taking things into our own hands.

"Grey Street" is the experience of one who has been enduring a dark night and is becoming weary of waiting for the assumed resolution. We don't hear about whether she ever finds it for herself, either in her attempts at prayer or in her general desire to get out of her current situation. That is left up to the listener to hope on her behalf, or to hear one's own life and faith struggles reflected. It could be that even the knowledge that others relate to this experience is a source of needed comfort in itself.

A GREY STREET PSALM

Just as one may be able to hear one's own life in one's favorite songs, there is one book of the Bible that has the capability to produce a similar result. The Psalms run the full gamut of human emotion, at times expressing thankfulness or contentment in times of prosperity or tranquility, at other times expressing doubt, anger, or sadness at God out of the belief that God is ignoring or doesn't care about what the writer is going through.

A good example of the latter is Psalm 42:

> As a deer longs for flowing streams, so my soul longs for you, O God.
> [2]My soul thirsts for God, for the living God. When shall I come and behold the face of God?
> [3]My tears have been my food day and night, while people say to me continually, "Where is your God?"
> [4]These things I remember, as I pour out my soul: how I went with the throng, and led them in procession to the house of God, with glad shouts and songs of thanksgiving, a multitude keeping festival.
> [5]Why are you cast down, O my soul, and why are you disquieted within me? Hope in God; for I shall again praise him, my help
> [6]and my God. My soul is cast down within me; therefore I remember you from the land of Jordan and of Hermon, from Mount Mizar.

⁷Deep calls to deep at the thunder of your cataracts; all your waves and your billows have gone over me.

⁸By day the Lord commands his steadfast love, and at night his song is with me, a prayer to the God of my life.

⁹I say to God, my rock, "Why have you forgotten me? Why must I walk about mournfully because the enemy oppresses me?"

¹⁰As with a deadly wound in my body, my adversaries taunt me, while they say to me continually, "Where is your God?"

¹¹Why are you cast down, O my soul, and why are you disquieted within me? Hope in God; for I shall again praise him, my help and my God. (Psalm 42)

The first verse of this psalm was once appropriated to write one of the most popular, reflective, and inspirational worship songs many Christian churches may sing on any given Sunday. However, the bulk of this psalm is anything but sweet and calming. The writer isn't painting a serene picture of a deer sipping water at a gentle stream's edge; rather, he or she is suffering from a throat dry from lack of water, lips cracked from thirst. Tears that happen to slip down the cheeks and into one's mouth serve as the only sustenance they will take. The question of "Where is your God?" rings as an accusation in one's ears, and the writer isn't afraid to ask the question themselves. They are at the end of their rope; the night couldn't be darker for them.

And yet, just as in "Grey Street," there is at least some hope peeking through the cracks. Perhaps this dark night will have a better ending; maybe there will yet be a way out. But as in the song, we are not given such a tidy ending. We are left to wonder whether the psalmist's hope ever paid off.

Biblical scholar Walter Brueggemann observes that most churches don't like psalms like this one because they acknowledge that life isn't as neat and tidy and comfortable as we'd like. Such psalms serve as invitations to admit when we are struggling and hurting; when we are wrestling with questions of where God is and whether God cares about what's happening to us. Psalms like these not only point out that the darkness exists, but they even embrace it as part of life in general and faith in particular.[7]

In Saint John of the Cross's dark night, there is hope that the person trying to feel their way through will eventually find a new and deepened way forward. This psalm expresses similar sentiments, interjecting hope between honesty about how miserable and lost the writer feels.

And this is also what we hear in songs like "Time Bomb" and "Grey Street." While Matthews is quite candid in interviews about what he thinks of certain conceptions of God, as well as the type of God he could accept if given definitive assurance that such a God exists, what he expresses through these songs is an experience that many know on an intimate level. Like the psalmist and the narrator of "Time Bomb," we may be yelling out of frustration that we have yet to find satisfactory answers to our faith questions. And like one going through Saint John's "dark night of the soul" and the main character of "Grey Street," we may keep praying even if we don't yet know whether it will do any good.

These songs help name these experiences for us. And we may still harbor a hope that our prayers will be answered.

---

7. Brueggemann, *The Message of the Psalms*, 53.

5

THE LIFE OF JESUS

During concerts, Dave Matthews sometimes introduces "Christmas Song" with a disclaimer: while the subject matter is Jesus, the song is not meant to be explicitly Christian. It's meant to express admiration for Jesus the man, while not necessarily endorsing the religion developed in his name.

While Matthews was raised Quaker, he long ago left behind that tradition's more metaphysical claims, including those about Jesus. This would include any sense that Jesus was the Son of God or had any divine attributes. However, Matthews seems to have retained some appreciation for who Jesus was as a person, and what he talked about and exemplified during his life. Matthews may say that he can find many commonalities with Jesus' words about love, forgiveness, mercy, and service to others, given that he often sings about these values in many of his other songs. For reasons already discussed in prior chapters, he just can't accept the idea of God being behind it. Nevertheless, as an exemplar of how Matthews believes humanity should treat one another, Jesus is one figure he lifts up as worth paying attention to.

A live acoustic version of "Christmas Song" is included on the band's earliest release, *Remember Two Things*. Other songs make passing references to Jesus, but they come nowhere close to the way this song focuses on his life. It's a slower, more reflective song, its tone like a lullaby. Matthews strums a descending chord progression both as the opening riff and through the verses.

The lyrics themselves provide a brief overview of Jesus' life; by the end refrain, the song has taken a journey through the basic story told in the Gospels, perhaps more closely resembling the first three (Matthew, Mark, and Luke), which share much of the same material between them. John, being the more mystical of the four contained in the Bible, doesn't find as much resonance in the song; this seems to reflect Matthews's own preferences and beliefs about what was most important about Jesus.

Matthews also skips around in Jesus' life a little, but begins with his birth as a song titled "Christmas Song" might. Only two of the four Gospels, Matthew and Luke, contain stories about Jesus' birth. Luke's is longer and more well-known, as it includes Jesus being laid in a manger in a stable, angels singing, and the shepherds visiting. The verse makes one reference to this version of the story as it mentions him lying among hay, but otherwise this verse seems to be culled more from Matthew's version, which is shorter and focuses more on Joseph's perspective rather than Mary's:

> Now the birth of Jesus the Messiah took place in this way. When his mother Mary had been engaged to Joseph, but before they lived together, she was found to be with child from the Holy Spirit. [19]Her husband Joseph, being a righteous man and unwilling to expose her to public disgrace, planned to dismiss her quietly. [20]But just when he had resolved to do this, an angel of the Lord appeared to him in a dream and said, "Joseph, son of David, do not be afraid to take Mary as your wife, for the child conceived in her is from the Holy Spirit. [21]She will bear a son, and you are to name him Jesus, for he will save his people from their sins." [22]All this took place to fulfill what had been spoken by the Lord through the prophet: [23]"Look, the virgin shall conceive and bear a son, and they shall name him Emmanuel," which means, "God is with us." [24]When Joseph awoke from sleep, he did as the angel of the Lord commanded him; he took her as his wife, [25]but

had no marital relations with her until she had borne a son; and he named him Jesus. (Matt 1:18–25)

"Christmas Song" mentions the Wise Men (or Magi), but not the other visitors. While many pageants and nativity scenes tend to include them in the manger with the shepherds and everyone else, the Magi only appear in the Gospel of Matthew's version, the popular theory being that they arrived later rather than right at Jesus' birth. Because Matthews includes these but not the others, it again reinforces that he's paying more attention to Matthew's version rather than Luke's.

Aside from these details, the most notable part of this opening verse might be how it describes Jesus himself. While many traditional carols emphasize Jesus' spiritual qualities and identity, even going so far as to insist that he doesn't cry, this song emphasizes his humanness. He is a baby just like any other: laughing, cooing, drooling, playing with his toes, needing to be fed and changed and have his neck and head properly supported when held.

As the result of this choice of emphasis, the listener is invited to give serious consideration to Jesus' humanity beyond the doctrinal statements, and even later claims that the Apostle Paul makes in his New Testament letters. What might change for Christian believers if we consider this side of Jesus, rather than giving it a wink before focusing back on how Jesus and God were connected? What does it mean that Jesus truly was human, rather than just seemed human?

For those who express appreciation for Jesus' teachings and don't have much use for the divine claims made about him, this is not an issue. But for those who believe that Jesus was human but also that God was somehow incarnate in him, the fact that he was once a vulnerable child who eventually went through puberty and other times of growth and struggle common to us all should have an impact on how one reads about him. As an embodied human being, Jesus had the full human experience, which demands that we sit with how he might have navigated that experience himself rather than jump to the later claims about his special status with God.

Continuing to follow the trajectory of Jesus' life, Matthews sings about how Jesus occasionally gave his mother fits while growing up. Out of the four Gospels, only Luke contains any story about Jesus' upbringing that takes place between his birth and the beginning of his ministry in adulthood:

> Now every year his parents went to Jerusalem for the festival of the Passover. [42]And when he was twelve years old, they went up as usual for the festival. [43]When the festival was ended and they started to return, the boy Jesus stayed behind in Jerusalem, but his parents did not know it. [44]Assuming that he was in the group of travelers, they went a day's journey. Then they started to look for him among their relatives and friends. [45]When they did not find him, they returned to Jerusalem to search for him. [46]After three days they found him in the temple, sitting among the teachers, listening to them and asking them questions. [47]And all who heard him were amazed at his understanding and his answers. [48]When his parents saw him they were astonished; and his mother said to him, "Child, why have you treated us like this? Look, your father and I have been searching for you in great anxiety." [49]He said to them, "Why were you searching for me? Did you not know that I must be in my Father's house?" [50]But they did not understand what he said to them. [51]Then he went down with them and came to Nazareth, and was obedient to them. His mother treasured all these things in her heart. [52]And Jesus increased in wisdom and in years, and in divine and human favor. (Luke 2:41–52)

If people of faith do choose to take the humanity of Jesus seriously, one might ask whether he ever had to be disciplined after reading this story. At any rate, this story seems to have been on Matthews's mind when he wrote this part of the song.

After that comes a reference to Mary Magdalene, and it echoes the often-repeated and mistaken belief that she was a prostitute. There is no mention of Mary Magdalene being such in the Bible. Instead, the Gospels state that she encountered Jesus because she'd been suffering from demonic possession:

Soon afterwards he went on through cities and villages, proclaiming and bringing the good news of the kingdom of God. The twelve were with him, [2]as well as some women who had been cured of evil spirits and infirmities: Mary, called Magdalene, from whom seven demons had gone out, [3]and Joanna, the wife of Herod's steward Chuza, and Susanna, and many others, who provided for them out of their resources. (Luke 8:1–3)

While the repetition of this claim may be erroneous, it seems mainly to serve what comes later in the song, which describes the rabble with which Jesus preferred to keep company. According to the Gospels, Jesus was often at odds with the religious leadership of his day due to his association with people who didn't have the highest societal standing. In various stories, he is eating with prostitutes and others who fall under the blanket term of "sinner," likely a reference to those who were considered ritually or socially unclean in some way, which would have carried with them a stigma that they were to be avoided.

According to the Gospels, Jesus often ignored these rules and regulations, touching lepers to heal them and sharing meals with people considered outsiders physically or spiritually. A typical example may be found in Luke 15:

Now all the tax collectors and sinners were coming near to listen to him. [2]And the Pharisees and the scribes were grumbling and saying, "This fellow welcomes sinners and eats with them." [3]So he told them this parable: [4]"Which one of you, having a hundred sheep and losing one of them, does not leave the ninety-nine in the wilderness and go after the one that is lost until he finds it? [5]When he has found it, he lays it on his shoulders and rejoices. [6]And when he comes home, he calls together his friends and neighbors, saying to them, 'Rejoice with me, for I have found my sheep that was lost.' [7]Just so, I tell you, there will be more joy in heaven over one sinner who repents than over ninety-nine righteous persons who need no repentance. [8]"Or what woman having ten silver coins, if she loses one of them, does not light a lamp, sweep the house, and search carefully until she finds it? [9]When she has found it, she calls together her friends and neighbors, saying, 'Rejoice with me, for I have found the coin that I had lost.' [10]Just so, I tell you, there is joy in the presence of the angels of God over one sinner who repents." (Luke 15:1–10)

This story begins with some religious leaders grumbling about who Jesus associates with: tax collectors (often considered betrayers of their own people by serving the Roman Empire, as well as embezzlers for taking way more than the empire needed to pocket themselves) and "sinners."

And yet Jesus welcomes them, eats with them, walks with them, and generally treats them as human beings just as worthy and deserving of God's love as those who dutifully adhere to their religious customs. As Matthews sings, they're all seeking something, regardless of their status in others' eyes. And by extension, that also includes us, whether we'd like to admit it or not.

Three other stanzas of the song focus on Jesus' death in some fashion. There is first some anticipation that Jesus will eventually do enough for the authorities to conspire together and justify removing him from public life. As his message grew in popularity, higher-ups would see it as more of a threat not just to established and proper religious practice, but also to the empire. He could inspire an uprising that civil authorities did not want to deal with, and so these two factions together (both really under the same Roman control, when it came down to it) believed they had good reason to erase the threat.

At one point, Matthews mentions what is traditionally known as the Last Supper, Jesus' final meal with the disciples before he was arrested. Again, in Matthew, Mark, and Luke, this meal was the traditional Passover observance, which recounted the Hebrew people's escape from Egypt in the book of Exodus and featured a meal hurriedly prepared and eaten beforehand. At various points in the Passover meal, those gathered would have drunk cups of wine and eaten unleavened bread as part of remembering what their ancestors went through when God liberated them from oppression and slavery.

In the Gospels, Jesus repurposed some of these culinary elements:

> While they were eating, Jesus took a loaf of bread, and after blessing it he broke it, gave it to the disciples, and said, "Take, eat; this is my body." [27]Then he took a cup, and after giving thanks he gave it to them, saying, "Drink from it, all of you; [28]for this is my blood of the covenant, which is poured out for many for the forgiveness of sins. [29]I tell you, I will never again drink of this fruit of the vine until that day when I drink it new with you in my Father's kingdom." [30]When they had sung the hymn, they went out to the Mount of Olives. (Matt 26:26–30)

For the purposes of the Passover, bread and wine were used as symbols that God was still with them, just as God was with those originally freed from Egyptian rule. Here Jesus tells his followers that now, they should use these as signs of his ongoing presence with them, no matter what happens next.

Matthews's knowledge of and appreciation for Jesus' life and teaching, including who he associated with, is quite clear in this song. However, he does also include an observation about how well people have been doing at following his example.

IN THE NAME OF JESUS

During a 1999 appearance on *VH1 Storytellers*, during which artists would not only play songs but also talk about the inspiration and meaning behind them, Matthews included "Christmas Song" in his setlist. While introducing the song, he stated that his inspiration for it came from a quote by Oscar Wilde: "If Christ was alive now, the one thing he wouldn't be is a Christian."[1]

The parts of "Christmas Song" not yet discussed seem to reflect Wilde's sentiments, as they have implications more for modern times than Jesus' life. The bridge of the song does mention Jesus being nailed to the cross, but it is in service of a commentary

1. Arnum, "Dave Matthews," para. 13.

on what has happened since that event. He imagines Jesus wondering what this might mean down the line; how people will interpret his life and death, not just for the sake of developing statements of faith for people to recite, but in terms of how those who call themselves followers will treat others.

Per Matthews in the song, Jesus shares his own sense of purpose, which is to enlighten and inspire; to show people how to live and how to treat one another, as well as perhaps provide a sense of hope. However, Jesus also voices a concern that the way people will receive and implement his message will be very different, and much more violent. Rather than bring hope, peace, and love to a hurting world, people will interpret or use Jesus' life for purposes such as angling for political power or governmental control, excluding those who are different, withholding help from the poor, hurting, and hungry, and using coercive and deadly force to convert or control. All of this in Jesus' name, as if invoking him will make it all okay, no matter how divorced from what he said it actually is.

Here is where Wilde's quote about Jesus probably not being a Christian comes in, because a lot of what self-identifies as "Christian" today seems to have very little to do with Jesus. Here was a man who during his life said things like "blessed are the merciful, for they will receive mercy" (Matt 5:7) and "love your enemy and pray for those who persecute you" (Matt 5:44). Here was a man who had no problem interacting with a Samaritan woman, despite his own ethno-religious background forbidding it (John 4:5–42) and who elsewhere made a Samaritan the hero of one of his best-known stories (Luke 10:25–37). Here was a man who taught about a father who welcomed back his irresponsible and disrespectful son with open arms, rather than shunning him, as the culture would have demanded (Luke 15:11–32).

Over the centuries, many calling themselves Christian have either forgotten or chosen to forego these sorts of teachings and the many instances in which Jesus hung out with prostitutes and "sinners"; who saw them all as people seeking love and redemption. As a result, many have experienced Jesus wielded at them like a weapon, rather than emulated in acts of kindness, welcome, and justice. This includes women, racial minorities, those who adhere to other faiths or no faith, and those who identify as LGBTQ. At times the blood spilled in the name of Jesus has been literal; at other times the wounds have been emotional or spiritual. My friend mentioned at the beginning of chapter 3 is one of thousands, if not millions, of examples.

And if Jesus were alive today, would he be welcome in most churches? Would he be able to bring his leper and prostitute friends with him without being turned away at the door, or avoided in the pews? If he served as guest preacher, could he stand up and talk about loving enemies without ridicule or accusations of being too offensive? Or could he challenge the values of today's empires without facing backlash or even being crucified all over again?

These questions lie behind Wilde's claim that Jesus probably wouldn't call himself a Christian. A lot of what Christians do nowadays looks and sounds little like the person who inspired the religion that bears his name.

BRAND VS. ETHICS

Both Matthews and Wilde are calling attention to the way people of faith approach Jesus; how they receive who he was, and how they live while striving to follow him. We could name more than two ways of doing so, but I'll focus on just two. Both profess a belief that Jesus was special, and worth listening to. Some from both groups may have faith that he was somehow God in human form, or otherwise had a unique role given to him by God. So what I am trying to name is less an issue of belief, and more one of action.

To begin, let's hear from Jesus one more time in the Gospel of Matthew:

> Beware of false prophets, who come to you in sheep's clothing but inwardly are ravenous wolves. [16]You will know them by their fruits. Are grapes gathered from thorns, or figs from thistles? [17]In the same way, every good tree bears good fruit, but the bad tree bears bad

fruit. [18]A good tree cannot bear bad fruit, nor can a bad tree bear good fruit. [19]Every tree that does not bear good fruit is cut down and thrown into the fire. [20]Thus you will know them by their fruits.

Not everyone who says to me, "Lord, Lord," will enter the kingdom of heaven, but only one who does the will of my Father in heaven. [22]On that day many will say to me, "Lord, Lord, did we not prophesy in your name, and cast out demons in your name, and do many deeds of power in your name?" [23]Then I will declare to them, "I never knew you; go away from me, you evildoers."

Everyone then who hears these words of mine and acts on them will be like a wise man who built his house on rock. [25]The rain fell, the floods came, and the winds blew and beat on that house, but it did not fall, because it had been founded on rock. [26]And everyone who hears these words of mine and does not act on them will be like a foolish man who built his house on sand. [27]The rain fell, and the floods came, and the winds blew and beat against that house, and it fell—and great was its fall! (Matt 7:15–27)

Jesus begins this passage by warning against false prophets, calling them "wolves in sheep's clothing." He refers to people who say, "Lord, Lord," but don't seem otherwise to be very interested in the term's implications for their lives. These are people who claim an affiliation with Jesus and who even address him directly, but don't exhibit any qualities in their daily actions and relationships that reflect who Jesus is.

How do we tell which from which? Jesus says, "you will know them by their fruits." Like a tree coming into season, a follower of Jesus should produce something good and life-giving and wonderful. Is the fruit juicy and delicious, or is it rotten? Is what one does in Jesus' name productive, or does it tear people down? Does it affirm and strengthen and inspire, or does it exclude and assert dominance and dehumanize? Does the fruit of someone calling themselves a Christian reflect the Jesus who befriended "sinners," or does it steer clear of them or beat them down in some way?

The people Jesus describes here are the first set I want to talk about: they are the ones who use him as a brand, as a name to slap on whatever they want to do, whether it looks much like what he did and taught in the Gospels or not. Often, this group will use Jesus to justify what they've already decided, rationalizing that they are on his team, wearing the uniform, and saying the right things about him.

In these instances, Jesus' likeness is a means of selling something, even if it is diametrically opposed to what he stood for. Politicians may do it to convince people to buy in to a policy that harms those in poverty or who are part of minority groups. Religious leaders may do it to justify excluding groups of people from participating in their faith communities. Individuals may do it to make themselves feel better about how they treat others on a daily basis. Jesus' example is nowhere to be found in these cases, only his name.

The second way of following Jesus is to give attention to his ethics. This takes his words more seriously, if not imperfectly. This way recognizes that what he taught was more than a series of nice things to pass the time while waiting for the events of the crucifixion to begin. After all, he had to have said or done something to have gotten the authorities' attention to begin with. So he gave hope to those downtrodden by religious rules and civil policy; he encouraged a different way of treating one another aside from the hierarchical system that people were familiar with, showing people a system of values based on love, forgiveness, peacemaking, and justice, rather than one of power, discrimination, coercion, and fear.

To follow this in any serious way, as more than a brand name, is to see people differently. It is to stand up for the troubled and struggling. It is to let the voiceless tell their story and take it seriously. It is to occasionally encounter resistance to a radically different way of interacting with the world.

An ethical approach to Jesus is to begin with the baby boy and see where his life takes him, rather than skip to the end or turn to what other Biblical writers say about him. It is to start with the difficult things he said, the surprising people he ate with, the countercultural way he saw people. It is to look at his vision of love spreading to everyone regardless of status or worth, and wondering how we can help bring it to fruition.

6

THE IMPORTANCE
OF NOW

If you walk the downtown area of Louisville, Kentucky, you might happen upon a plaque on a street corner that, at a glance, might seem unusual. Why would someone have placed a plaque here, of all places; what sort of special significance could such a location have? A closer look will reveal that it commemorates a pivotal moment in the life of Trappist monk and spiritual writer Thomas Merton, who wrote about a transcendent experience he had while standing there one day.

He shares this experience in his book *Conjectures of a Guilty Bystander*, which occurred at the corner of Walnut and Fourth. He describes observing the busyness around him, such as the people going to work or running errands, and becoming overwhelmed with a sense of deep connection to and love for them all.[1]

With Merton's experience came the realization that a sense of the holy or transcendent is not reserved for places like houses of worship or monasteries. Nor do we have to wait until we enter whatever we believe about the life that follows this one to feel or acknowledge God's presence. Rather, the ordinary moments of our

1. Erickson, "On a Busy Street Corner," para. 2.

days are just as infused with the spiritual and sacred, if we just pay attention.

But we may find it difficult to give such attention to what's right in front of us. After all, much like the people around Merton that day, as well as Merton himself, we're all going somewhere. They had places to be, purchases to make, appointments to keep, responsibilities to satisfy. Even Merton perhaps believed that he needed to get his own obligations out of the way so that he could get back to his abbey, and to the work of prayer that surely was more important than what he was doing on a street corner.

But one moment of slowing down and seeing what is right in front of us can change everything. And it may be that you've had such moments in your own life but wouldn't describe them with the same language as Merton, even if the experience was similar.

Have you ever had a moment when you were with a group of friends (and maybe also strangers), and were struck by a feeling of having a kinship with them all? Or a time when the first bite of a special meal overcame your senses and you needed to pause and savor every time you chewed it? Or when the sight of a mountain range or the ocean or a sunset paralyzed you with wonder and peace?

You may or may not reference God relative to these experiences, but you may nevertheless remember such times for yourself. They were times that came with a special sense that you are a part of something beyond just your own life, but which also reminded you of how precious and amazing all of existence is. They're the sorts of moments that remind you not to look too far beyond what's right in front of you, because what's right in front of you carries the potential to be awe-inspiring.

Dave Matthews expressed a similar view during an interview, where he shared his view that we should pay more attention to all the small things we encounter every day that inspire wonder. He mentions things like a child laughing or the way the wind moves, or how people go out of their way to help each other. According to Matthews, we tend not to spend enough time noticing these seemingly insignificant or typical parts of existence that we see so often.

If we had a greater capacity for awareness and wonder, we could also have a greater capacity for appreciating the here and now. And if we had a greater capacity for appreciating the here and now, we'd realize the opportunities before us for greater participation and immersion in the possibilities in our present moment.[2]

In Matthews's view, any kind of religious devotion or spirituality that takes our minds or hearts too far away from what is happening right now is too disembodied to be useful. Such a view of the world neglects all the possibilities of intentional connection that we can make to our immediate surroundings—the ways we can feel amazement or relationship with everything around us, and the ways the divine shows up during meals and community engagement, at work, with family, in nature, and on street corners. If we practice forms of spirituality that remove our attention from that potential, we miss out on ways we may forge greater understanding of how intertwined we are with it all, and how each present moment is an opportunity for experience rather than a barrier to something we want to do at some point in the future.

NOT PROMISED TOMORROW

"Tripping Billies" was the fifth single off the band's third album, *Crash*. The song is high energy and features a memorable riff played by LeRoi Moore on saxophone and Boyd Tinsley on violin that repeats itself throughout. There is some dispute as to the origin of the song's title, with even Matthews himself having offered different explanations at times.

Despite the varied explanations of its name, the foundational experience that led to the song's composition was an acid trip that Matthews had on the beach with friends in South Africa. During an unaired portion of *VH1 Storytellers*, Matthews gave a brief recap of this time where as soon as he accepted the drug and ingested it,

2. Q on CBC, "Dave Matthews," 35:12–37:10.

he regretted it, even though by that point there was nothing he could do but go through with it.[3]

Even if the song's inspiration was a hallucinogenic experience, its overall focus is more on seizing the day and living each moment to the fullest, which is a common theme of the band's music. In the earliest lines, Matthews seems to be alluding to his beach experience, and he chooses to remember small details like bees stinging him and the company of his friends while they were together. The group is enjoying themselves despite small discomforts.

The other verses are just as specific in their imagery, forsaking broad themes for something more vivid and personal. From picturing shadows on the sand to accessories the attendees wore to the campfire and dancing to the specific form of imbibement enjoyed, the party depicted in this song becomes very concrete. And coupled with the upbeat and frantic tempo and interplay between instruments, to listen to the song is to almost be on the beach yourself. Not only that, but the song accomplishes its goal of putting the listener right in the moment, just as its partygoers are enjoying the evening without worrying what the next day will bring.

At one point, Matthews wonders why anyone would want to hurry away too quickly from this party atmosphere, where people are laughing, dancing, drinking, and being together. Here we are, not a care in the world, letting our minds wander wherever this time takes us. There's no concern about an early wakeup time or any kind of work or responsibility that the next day might bring. Instead, there is only the joy and relaxation of what's happening now.

Matthews also repeats a paraphrase of a line that appears several times in the Bible. The first appearance of this line comes in Isaiah, where the people are ignoring what God wants them to do:

> [12]In that day the Lord God of hosts called to weeping and mourning, to baldness and putting on sackcloth; [13]but instead there was joy and festivity, killing oxen and slaughtering sheep, eating meat and drinking wine. "*Let*

3. Arnum, "Dave Matthews," paras. 11–12.

us eat and drink, for tomorrow we die." (Isa 22:12–13, italics mine)

The second instance comes in 1 Corinthians, where the writer, Paul, is in an argument with that faith community about the impact of the resurrection on everyday living:

> [32]If with merely human hopes I fought with wild animals at Ephesus, what would I have gained by it? If the dead are not raised, "*Let us eat and drink, for tomorrow we die.*" [33]Do not be deceived: "Bad company ruins good morals." [34]Come to a sober and right mind, and sin no more; for some people have no knowledge of God. I say this to your shame. (1 Cor 15:32–34, italics mine)

Given the context of this phrase's use in both passages, one may be led to conclude that it only conveys a spirit of hedonism and irresponsibility; that it reflects an attitude of vanity and short-sightedness that revels in bad behavior. Due to how it is mentioned in Scripture, many Christians may view this phrase as beyond redeeming, as it is only ever used as part of a critique of how not to live faithfully; an indictment of carelessness and as part of a call to wake up and get right.

Is this how Matthews uses it? And could the encouragement to eat and drink because we could very well die tomorrow ever be part of a healthy spiritual outlook?

Consider again the imagery of "Tripping Billies:" a party on a beach complete with drinks, a campfire, dancing, and an overall outlook that we shouldn't leave too soon; that we should linger and enjoy this time for what it is. If we couple what we hear and can picture from the song with Matthews's thoughts shared at the beginning of the chapter about wondering and savoring and connecting to our immediate surroundings, we may be able to interpret this phrase in a more constructive way.

Again, the song makes it a point to notice the little things: the presence of insects, the construction of bracelets, the flicker of a fire, the taste of cocktails. There are times when we might have the chance to pay attention to one or more of these sorts of things in our own lives, but how often do we take advantage of doing so? How could slowing down to notice the small things that contribute to our day help nurture our sense of wonder about the world and, if we are so inclined, the transcendent power that created it or is present within it?

Each of these carries the potential to reveal something to us about how special and strange the world is, apart from what might happen even an hour from now. As Merton discovered on a Louisville street corner, the mundane things we take for granted are part of a spiritual experience that we are already having, if we give them their proper due and acknowledge their contribution to a rich existence where the transcendent is all around us now, rather than waiting for us in the next life.

Tomorrow our lives might be over. But before then, there's something of beauty and truth to which we could be giving our attention in everything happening to us.

CELEBRATING LIFE—A PSALM

Given how various Biblical writers tended to respond to the phrase "eat and drink, for tomorrow we die," one might conclude that Biblical encouragement to take pleasure in this life are few and far between. The two examples in Isaiah and 1 Corinthians are more concerned with approaching life—including its joys—in a more serious way, and the authors of these scriptural passages don't believe that this phrase advocates for doing so.

One of the best examples of giving thanks for the more enjoyable things in life comes in Psalm 104:

> You make springs gush forth in the valleys; they flow between the hills,
> [11]giving drink to every wild animal; the wild asses quench their thirst.
> [12]By the streams the birds of the air have their habitation; they sing among the branches.
> [13]From your lofty abode you water the mountains; the earth is satisfied with the fruit of your work.

[14]You cause the grass to grow for the cattle, and plants for people to use, to bring forth food from the earth,

[15]and wine to gladden the human heart, oil to make the face shine, and bread to strengthen the human heart.

[16]The trees of the Lord are watered abundantly, the cedars of Lebanon that he planted.

[17]In them the birds build their nests; the stork has its home in the fir trees.

[18]The high mountains are for the wild goats; the rocks are a refuge for the coneys.

[19]You have made the moon to mark the seasons; the sun knows its time for setting.

[20]You make darkness, and it is night, when all the animals of the forest come creeping out.

[21]The young lions roar for their prey, seeking their food from God.

[22]When the sun rises, they withdraw and lie down in their dens.

[23]People go out to their work and to their labor until the evening.

[24]O Lord, how manifold are your works! In wisdom you have made them all; the earth is full of your creatures. (Psalm 104:10–24)

This psalm is a free-flowing, stream-of-consciousness expression of appreciation for everything that God has made, from plants to animals to rocks to water to the times of day and night. It is a psalm of wonder at the vastness of creation and the interconnectedness of nature, where God cares for and provides for everything that God has made. There were no street corners in those days, but the psalmist found ways to be in awe of everything around him anyway.

A closer look at this psalm shows that not only does the writer show amazement at each created thing itself, but also how it benefits other parts of God's order. Springs and streams flowing through valleys and hills are wondrous to watch, but they also give drink and habitation to various kinds of animals. Grass and trees are vast and majestic in their own right, but cattle also may eat them, or birds may nest in them. Various forms of plants may provide food and nourishment for humanity, but they also may be used for wine, oil, and bread that not only serve pragmatic functions, but pleasurable and aesthetic ones as well.

This psalmist is in wonder and confusion at how immense and far-reaching and interrelated everything in this life is. And observing creation in this way not only sparks amazement, but also gratitude for how living beings may enjoy them. If this writer had been on a beach in South Africa, he may have added sand, the ocean, fire, the sunset, pineapple, music, laughter, bees, and tequila to his list. Some of these sustain us in practical ways, while others enrich life beyond our basic needs. Just as the psalmist celebrates both in his psalm, so might he do so in other situations.

Psalm 104 chooses to view creation as a gift to be enjoyed, rather than a means to an end or a holdover until death comes calling. It shows us that eating, drinking, and being merry is permissible, and even encouraged. It celebrates that there is so much in this life worth paying attention to and leaning into as wonderful aspects of being together, as part of what God has made.

Are there ways to abuse such a gift? Of course. Isaiah and Paul had to call out several instances where people were ignoring other aspects of this life's needs in favor of their own enjoyment. But when such moments come as they did for Merton, where we realize how incredible a gift all of existence is and how we are welcome to participate fully in its delights as well as its concerns, we deepen our relationships with the transcendent, with other aspects of creation with whom we are inextricably linked, and with ourselves.

Eating, drinking, and merriment help give depth and enrichment to life, highlighting the gift of each moment. Why be so quick to leave when there is so much potential to sit on beaches or stand on street corners, and to fall ever more in love with everything around us?

7

TEMPTATION, ADDICTION, AND DETACHMENT

I wasn't much of a drinker in college. I'd fallen in with a group of Christians very evangelical and conservative in outlook, and alcohol was generally frowned upon in that circle of people. In their view, to engage in drinking was to damage one's witness to the rest of the campus. It somehow translated to a loss of credibility when trying to prove to others the genuineness of one's belief and the truth of the gospel. This conflation of teetotalling with Christian faithfulness has been around for quite some time, and for a while I bought into it. Admittedly, I went along with it more to avoid the judgmental gaze of my fellow believers than out of any wholehearted belief that abstaining was what Jesus would have done, wedding at Cana in John 2 notwithstanding.

Once I finally moved on from my undergraduate years and my friendships with several of the primary enforcers of this "no alcohol = good discipleship" view disintegrated, I was finally free to explore what I thought I'd been missing up until that point in my life. Believe it or not, my seminary years became the time when I'd break out and indulge in all manner of drinking after hours, my early twenties fast becoming what my college career, stereotypically, was to many of my peers.

I credit my previous repression with what tended to transpire on the weekends during that time, which frequently saw me in friends' apartments, out in pubs, or even alone in my own place experimenting, taste-testing, exploring that which I thought was forbidden to me in the prior phase of my life. In addition, I was on my own in a big city, five hundred miles away from everyone I knew, and dealing with a deep sense of loneliness during a time of tremendous adjustment. Due to this combination of factors, during these weekend sessions, I found it difficult to find an off switch; a point where I knew enough was enough. Rum and Coke was a favorite, as were most beers and wines. I occasionally dabbled in martinis, though only on special trips to certain places around town.

Mind you, this never affected or impeded my classwork or relationships, so I don't know that one could classify my imbibement as a full-blown addiction. But there was nevertheless something unhealthy about my love for and attraction to alcohol around that time. My friends recognized it, and in sober moments I could see it as well, but it wasn't enough to get me to slow down. Maybe that qualifies as addiction after all.

Early in my final year of school, a group of us were gathered in the common area of our apartment building. The drink of choice that night was wine, and the bottles seemed to keep appearing on the table after others had been emptied. Again, I had no stopping point, holding out my glass for one refill after another. We eventually dispersed, and I stumbled down to my room to begin sleeping it off.

This time, however, something felt different. My mind was the cloudiest that it had ever felt, and my ability to concentrate on the simplest things was non-existent. My body was also reacting in a way I'd never experienced, and it wasn't before long that I found myself with my arms curled around my toilet, all the wine of the evening making its second, much less appetizing appearance.

I slept in fits and starts on the floor of the bathroom that night, my wife feeling the need to check on me every so often. The next day was spent nursing the worst headache I'd ever had, and the smallest movements caused me to wonder whether another rush to the bathroom was imminent.

This was the one and only time I'd ever experience that level of drunkenness, and I resolved never again even to come close to having that much in one sitting. I knew that I didn't want to feel that out of control any more, much less go through the aftereffects. I took steps to cut back; to identify my off switch, to avoid endangering myself the way I did that night.

I don't share this as any sort of exceptional or extreme case that differs from that of others. In truth, relative to the stories others could tell, mine is much less severe, the damage minimal in comparison. But I can say that I now know for myself when enough is enough, and I have learned the risks of going overboard with something that to me tasted so good and helped me feel so free. I have other healthier ways to feel like that now. But many others have not been so fortunate to find that for themselves.

In his extensive writing on addiction and recovery, Daniel Maurer observes that, from his own experience in pursuing sobriety, a willingness to be honest with himself has been key to his own wellness. In fact, he admits, drinking and drugs were for him a way to avoid such honesty about what might be wrong in his own life: "Alcohol and drugs were a perfect match for not thinking about my life, or anything else. It's easy to forget when you're blasted."[1]

Looking back, I can see my desire to forget lingering bitter feelings from my college years, and the fact that I wasn't dealing very well with the transition to my new surroundings. I can name the ways these factors for which I hadn't identified good coping skills (as well as my avoidance of processing their effects) contributed to my overindulgence. The issues that lead us to numb ourselves in such ways may vary, but that we may seek out unhealthy mechanisms to shield ourselves from some honest self-reflection is much more common.

1. Maurer, *Endure*, xii.

Dave Matthews may like to sing about seizing the day, making the most out of one's life, and living in the present moment as much as one can. But he just as often explores the dangers in taking eating and drinking too far: when we do so not to savor life, but to avoid living it.

AN APPETITE THAT WON'T QUIT

"Too Much" was Dave Matthews Band's first single off their third album *Crash*. The song has an upbeat, frantic feel to it, and begins with a violin riff that repeats as an interlude between verses. The accompanying video features the band playing on a bare stage interspersed with scenes of men in Coke bottle glasses and bowler hats consuming every piece of food and drink that they can get their hands on.

That imagery reflects the content of the song, which focuses on the singer's desire to always acquire more no matter how much he already has. Matthews himself has said of the song that enjoyment of life has given way to consuming it in an unhealthy manner.[2]

In other words, the narrator can't find his off switch. He seems to have no self-awareness regarding when enough is enough. In fact, there is no such thing as enough. He brags about having more possessions than anyone can count, and expresses that not only does he love acquiring more, but he is somehow entitled to it.

As the song progresses, he adds a new wrinkle to the way he's accumulating what he has. At first the narrator is expressing a general need and intention to get as much as he can, but he eventually introduces a new idea: taking from others in order to get more. He demands that others perform for him and states that he's going to push boundaries to encroach on others and take what is theirs for himself. He expresses no remorse or hesitation about this, only the sense that nobody else's feelings or needs matter but his own. The narrator uses a generous amount of hyperbole to illustrate just

2. Delancey, *Step Into the Light*, 170.

how strong his compulsion is. No matter the cost to himself or to others, he still wants more.

These sentiments show the potential side effects that compulsive greed and overconsumption can have on others. Those who rig systems to secure greater wealth for themselves often do so at the expense of those in lower tax brackets. Those who struggle with addiction take advantage of others' kindness and trust to pursue their next fix. Unchecked indulgence often hurts or takes away from others, whether it is tangible acquisition of what should or could have gone to someone else, the emotional toll that wears on those from whom it is taken, or someone's needs which are neglected for one's own benefit.

What happens to people who don't have an off switch on their appetites? Sometimes they end up on the bathroom floor wondering if they have alcohol poisoning. Sometimes they exhaust relationships and burn bridges. Sometimes they take opportunities that for them are basic needs, but for others are luxurious. Sometimes their consumption leads to physical or mental disease that causes them to finally seek help, or which ultimately kills them. Their compulsion to keep going becomes fatal.

THE TEACHER'S "BATHROOM FLOOR" MOMENT

The book of Ecclesiastes is not a part of the Bible that is as well-known. But it frequently offers insightful, if not often depressing, commentary on the purpose of daily life. The author, sometimes thought to be King Solomon and often referred to as the Teacher, is despairing about how pointless his existence feels. Mind you, Solomon was one of the wealthiest and most successful monarchs of the classic Israel kingdom, so to hear him, of all people, come to the repeated realization that much of humanity's work doesn't matter in the grand scheme of things might lead the reader of this book to despair themselves.

At one point, the Teacher shares this reflection:

I said to myself, "Come now, I will make a test of pleasure; enjoy yourself." But again, this also was vanity. [2]I said of laughter, "It is mad," and of pleasure, "What use is it?" [3]I searched with my mind how to cheer my body with wine—my mind still guiding me with wisdom—and how to lay hold on folly, until I might see what was good for mortals to do under heaven during the few days of their life. [4]I made great works; I built houses and planted vineyards for myself; [5]I made myself gardens and parks, and planted in them all kinds of fruit trees. [6]I made myself pools from which to water the forest of growing trees. [7]I bought male and female slaves, and had slaves who were born in my house; I also had great possessions of herds and flocks, more than any who had been before me in Jerusalem. [8]I also gathered for myself silver and gold and the treasure of kings and of the provinces; I got singers, both men and women, and delights of the flesh, and many concubines. [9]So I became great and surpassed all who were before me in Jerusalem; also my wisdom remained with me. [10]Whatever my eyes desired I did not keep from them; I kept my heart from no pleasure, for my heart found pleasure in all my toil, and this was my reward for all my toil. [11]Then I considered all that my hands had done and the toil I had spent in doing it, and again, all was vanity and a chasing after wind, and there was nothing to be gained under the sun. (Eccl 2:1–11)

In the first line of this passage, the Teacher is setting out to undertake a "test of pleasure," to see whether the accumulation of treasures and the satisfying of whatever craving comes to him will be enough to meet his longing for a fulfilled life. He takes "enjoy yourself" to the most extreme and perhaps absurd level that he can in order to see whether this will bring him deep happiness. Whereas the narrator of "Too Much" argues that feeding his appetite no matter the cost is the way to enjoyment, the Teacher wonders how true that mode of thinking really is.

So the Teacher does much of what the narrator does: he drinks wine, builds houses, plants vineyards and fruit trees, creates gardens and parks, digs pools, expands his herds and flocks, gathers all manner of precious minerals, fills his court with enter-tainment and his bedroom with concubines. Whatever he wants, he ventures out and gets. And for at least a little while, all this work and the resulting rewards seem to placate him; they truly seem to give him pleasure.

But after further consideration, the Teacher realizes how fleeting that pleasure is. Once he stops all his building and gather-ing and consuming and is left to his thoughts, he's right back where he started. If he'd continued all these pursuits, perhaps the pleasure would have continued as well; the endorphins would have kept flowing and he'd have felt contented. But upon stopping, he real-izes something of the temporal nature of the happiness that these actions provide.

Will the narrator of "Too Much" come to a similar revelation if he ever pauses his accumulation? And if he does, what will hap-pen to him then?

TRAPPED BY ADDICTION

"Rhyme & Reason" is the fourth track on the band's breakthrough album, *Under the Table and Dreaming*. It's one of the darker songs on the album, though the musical arrangement is upbeat enough that the listener might not feel bogged down by the content. If the narrator of "Too Much" is bragging about an insatiable appetite causing him to bulldoze his way through everything to get what he wants, "Rhyme & Reason" could be the same narrator further down the road after finally stopping to consider all that he's done: the resulting burdens and collateral damage that his behavior has caused have caught up with him.

The song features someone feeling trapped, although it takes a while for this person to name the cause. It begins with an image of the narrator in extreme discomfort: his head is throbbing and his thoughts are jumbled together. He wants so badly for his suffer-ing to end, but he doesn't know how to do that other than to keep doing what he's been doing already.

The thoughts and cravings churning within him cause the narrator to conclude that he doesn't think he'll ever feel relief until he's dead. Whatever cycle he's stuck in, he's hopeless that he can ever break out of it. The song doesn't do much at first to describe what that cycle might be, but we're led to believe that he is feeling such deep torment over it that he doesn't believe will ever end.

The narrator continues describing what we could call symptoms related to addiction or withdrawal. He's in so deep and perhaps has gone long enough since his last fix that he wonders about—and seems to suffer some pre-emptive shame over—what he might have to do to secure his next one. He even gives a hint that he realizes some of the damage he's caused himself and others as he recognizes how alone he is; he may finally be willing to be honest with himself about needing to change.

It's not until almost the very end where the narrator explicitly mentions substance abuse, and one question that may arise is: what came first, his feelings of being lost and disordered, or the drinking and drugs? Did something in his life that he didn't want to face cause him to mask it behind addictive habits, or did the smoking and alcohol and the resulting cravings for more lead to it? Did he first seek satisfaction elsewhere because he didn't want to be honest about something in his life, or is he now indulging in something that will keep him in perpetual denial and self-sabotage?

Whether one perpetrated the other or they assisted each other in some way, the narrator is now admitting that his unhealthy obsessions have led him to this point. There is a sliver of hope in the last line, as he reaches out to some unknown friend, asking them to take his chosen method of using away. What will happen next? The song doesn't say. But this could be the breakthrough that the person voicing his struggles needs.

Like the Teacher, our narrator knows what his overindulgence has cost him. For most of the song, it seems as if he's aware even while giving no indication that he can or wants to escape. The appeal to his friend suggests that maybe he does believe that he can change, but as long as the road has been for him so far, the road to recovery will be as long, if not longer.

MODERATION AND DETACHMENT

Ignatius of Loyola was a Catholic priest, founder of what we know today as the Jesuit order, and composer of an extensive guide of prayer practices known as the Spiritual Exercises. In his initial set of annotations describing the Exercises' underlying principles and ways to guide interested practitioners through them, he at one point focuses on the ways we develop unhealthy relationships with people, objects, or habits. However, Ignatius adds that God works with those experiencing such an all-consuming attachment to something that only brings disorder for them, in order to dissuade them from it and back toward an orientation to what is good and life-giving and wonder-inspiring.[3]

These "disordered attachments," as Ignatius calls them, could be any number of things. For my younger self, it was an overreliance on the numbing effects of alcohol. For the narrator of "Too Much," it's whatever he can consume no matter the price to self or others. For the Teacher, it could have been the building and gathering of vast wealth and riches had he not stopped to ponder their true worth. For the narrator of "Rhyme & Reason," it had been various forms of drugs even after his realization that he had to keep pursuing them to quiet his inner turmoil.

For Ignatius, the character of these disordered attachments is fairly straightforward: the obtaining and keeping of something, not to grow spiritually or to benefit others, but in the service of one's own pleasures or advancement, regardless of the personal or relational cost.[4] The term "disordered attachment" is apt, because it implies that we have an unhealthy predisposition to maintain the advantage or high that it gives us; we'll do what we can to protect and nurture it because we've come to depend on it for meaning

---

3. Ivens, *Understanding the Spiritual Exercises*, 15.
4. Ivens, *Understanding the Spiritual Exercises*, 15.

or relief or security. We are hopelessly attached to it physically, mentally, or spiritually.

But this attachment has a certain character that is, in the long term, not beneficial for us. It may seem so, but we don't see how our preoccupation with it is causing harm to us or to others. It is causing disorder, even if it feels like it helps us remain stable and on track. While we may begin as the figure in "Too Much," we may have our own "bathroom floor" moment where we come to ourselves much like the Teacher or narrator in "Rhyme & Reason," and begin to wonder whether we can start being honest with ourselves about what we've become and what we need to become healthy again.

There are many healthy ways to enjoy life. Some people may have a tendency to view any pleasure as evil or harmful due to its possible addictive effects. Likewise, we may not see how our enjoyment veers into destructive behavior if we don't identify our off switch, or aren't honest with ourselves about what such pleasures might be helping us avoid.

There is a difference between life abundant and life overindulgent. The former features moderation, self-awareness, and trust in and from others to maintain healthy relationships with the forms of pleasure we choose. Life overindulgent has no such boundaries or assessment, and may veer into disordered attachment that one day may see us on a bathroom floor or otherwise feeling trapped in one's own despair or habits, wondering how we got here or how to get out.

This balance is different for everyone, but the need for honesty with ourselves and others to maintain it is the same. For what reason are we taking yet another drink, making yet another purchase, or seeking yet another temporary relationship? What might we be using it to avoid? What would happen if we stopped to ask?

8

FACING OUR
OWN IDENTITY

How do you answer when somebody asks, "Who are you?"
How do you conceptualize the question to begin with? Do
you ever fumble when you answer, or do you have to think for a
few moments first? Are you ever at a complete loss for words when
asked? What does it mean to be asked this question?

We tend to have several ready-made answers. First, we may
respond with whatever our job or career is; whatever we do for
a living. We may first know ourselves—or feel we may best be
known or appreciated by others—by the role we play as part of
working society. So when asked who we are we might answer that
we're a teacher, or a nurse, or a manager, or a barista. We've been
conditioned to make our method of income one of our primary
identifiers.

A second possible way we may answer the question is by re-
sponding with who we are in relationship to someone else. "I'm
Frank's spouse." "I'm Nancy's parent." "I'm Joe's brother." This may
help if the asker knows who Frank or Nancy or Joe are, or if they've
long known or worked with them, and are just meeting you. But
this response carries with it the implication that we may be known

primarily by who we are with. Answering this way makes sense when attending your partner's work party or your child's school play, but how well does it capture who you are outside of those situations?

WHAT IF IT HAD ALL BEEN DIFFERENT?

"Dancing Nancies" is the sixth track on the band's major debut, *Under the Table and Dreaming*. It explores the question of "Who are you?" in a different way, where Matthews openly wonders whether he could have been born into a different situation. He considers whether circumstances could have turned out some other way, and what it could have led to if they had. In one of Matthews's better-known explanations of the song, he described an experience of hitchhiking in South Africa where he began wondering what he was going to do with his life, and what he could be.[1]

To many readers and listeners, Matthew's questions may sound familiar because we've asked them ourselves. And it may be that, even after selecting a path and following what we know we need to do to achieve our goals, we may wonder what could have happened if we'd decided differently, or if certain doors hadn't opened for us, or whether we could still switch trajectories even now.

Matthews begins the song by rattling off a series of different professions that he wonders if he could have had. He doesn't seem to aspire to any of these, but instead lists them as a few examples of hundreds of possibilities. Rather than being who he ended up as, could he have been someone completely different? The unspoken question at this point is, what else would have had to happen for each of those to have occurred? Here is a person looking in the mirror wondering who they are and struggling with the answer or lack of one. He is still young, but already seems to feel trapped by whatever kind of life he's leading, and the prospects of becoming the person he wants to be seem already to be fading further into his rearview.

1. Martell, *Music for the People*, 40.

Whether we've chosen a path for our lives or career, whether we're still deciding, or whether we're in the middle of pursuing a goal, we may yet have questions at the back of our minds wondering if we've chosen correctly, or if there's still time to change. We may even drill down to those elements beyond our control, like if our parents had met different people, or what could have happened if we'd have had more fortunate opportunities, or if our families weren't as well-connected. If even one of the million little things that added up to where we are had gone a different way, who could we have wound up becoming?

Eventually, the protagonist accepts that he is who he is thanks to upbringing, economics, education, and other factors—but who is he? All these intangible and uncontrollable influences have created a person, but who is that person beyond what his family and surrounding community has made? How will he react to or transcend the cards he's been given? How would he describe himself beyond the series of labels thrust upon him? What would he say about who he is, where he's going, who he wants to be in his own words?

There comes a point when the narrator accepts that he doesn't need to have it all completely figured out, especially at such a young age. While he doesn't give up asking these important questions related to his identity, he can at least loosen his grip enough to take joy in his immediate surroundings: watching the clouds or the stars, catching raindrops on his tongue, dancing until he collapses. He seeks a balance between finding out who he is while also trying not to let his search cripple his spirit. Such a thing is not easy for everyone to achieve, and even the person in this song seems to vacillate between such joy and darker moments of self-doubt.

Again, such a struggle may be familiar to most people. There are times when the questions weigh heavily, and times when we're able to put off such deep worry to enjoy the process of exploration. Some may find such a journey of self-discovery to be exciting, but it may also reveal truths about mistakes made and opportunities lost. At times, we may look up at the sky, able to put the smallness of ourselves in perspective. At other times, we may wonder whether clarity for ourselves may ever come.

BEYOND THE EASY ANSWERS

If you stripped away the two handy ways to answer the question "Who are you?" (career and relationships), what would be left to say? How might we think about the question if we couldn't talk about our work or relationships, the parts we play for others?

We may begin to answer the question "Who are you?" by looking back on where we've been and who and what has been most influential in raising and shaping us in our growing and maturing years. Whether we realize it or not, such factors continue to have an impact on how we see ourselves, and how we interact with others.

We do not develop in a vacuum. Instead, we are part of a vast and complex network of relationships, communities, and experiences. These leave impressions on us in ways we often are not aware of, and it takes self-reflection (and maybe a good therapist or spiritual director) to help us see them more clearly.

Here is a brief rundown of several such influences on our sense of identity.

Our first experiences happen in relationship to our families. We are born into systems where our parents and siblings have roles to play, and we eventually learn our own identity within that system. If that system is mostly supportive, where people are mindful of and attentive to each other's needs, then we may move from dependence to independence in a relatively healthy way.[2]

Even in healthy families, however, we pick up on social cues from those we live with and learn our role in the family in response to them. For instance, if the wife and mother is prone to withdrawing during conflict, we may find ourselves playing the role of stepping in to facilitate instead. If the father figure has a temper that boils over at minor provocations, we might take on the identity of peacemaker or pleaser to calm things down. These roles follow us into later life where we continue to play them out in other relationships. Through our families, we have been programmed to

2. Hamman, *Becoming a Pastor*, 24.

react to people and situations in a certain way; to take on a sense of identity that follows us into adulthood.[3]

Similar to how our families influence identity is the impact of other social relationships. If your school experience was anything like mine, you were made to attend more than one assembly or drug awareness talk describing the dangers of peer pressure, with encouragements to not simply go along with what your closest friends are doing even if it brings rejection. Overall, the concept of how our friends try to influence us growing up tends to be framed negatively, as if going along with what they want always leads to substance abuse or other destructive actions.

Considered more neutrally, relationships with friends are the first ones we make beyond our families as we begin to pull away and discover who we are without or beyond them. I recall a conversation during my son's earliest years where someone commented to me, "Once they start school, they're not yours anymore." This person meant that once we begin interacting with kids our own age, we begin cross-pollinating behaviors and attitudes and experimenting with who we are in a world that turns out to be bigger than our home life.

Naturally, in these years, we want to do what our friends are doing. At this point, learning our identity becomes a process similar to that which plays out in families, where we ask, "Who am I relative to others my age?" At times it means taking on others' behavior, and at times it means rejecting it. At times it means being reined in by watchful parental figures and other trusted adult guides, at times learning by trial and error, and at times forging one's own way.[4] Peer groups are the next circle of our finding out who we are.

Perhaps the most overarching and complicated factor that plays a role in our sense of identity is the larger culture in which we are raised. By culture, I mean the general setting where our lives and socialization take place. I could spend the rest of the book

---

3. Gross, "Like Parent, Like Child," para. 8.
4. Ulene, "A Teen's Friends," para. 6.

attempting to describe the many factors at play here, but I will instead present a brief overview.

The families and peer groups we are a part of are embedded within a much larger framework of values and characteristics that, much like what I have already mentioned, often go unexamined. This includes the understood ways people interact in public places, how people dress, how people speak, the ways disputes are managed, what religious beliefs may enjoy privileged expression at public events without being questioned, and even what businesses enjoy greater success. All of this (and much more) makes up the culture where our lives take place.

There is an old adage that says that if you ask a fish how the water is, it will reply, "What water?" We are often the fish swimming in the waters of our surrounding culture, unaware that its particulars are different from what we may find elsewhere. We often assume that our waters are "normal," or we may believe that they are the way things should be wherever we go. For instance, someone whose life is embedded in a predominately white small town will have quite an adjustment if they move to a larger, more racially diverse city, and vice versa. The unspoken norms between these two cultural spaces are very different from each other.

One culture is not superior or inferior, and this is to say nothing of how, over time, we may be able to transcend one culture to understand or live in another (with many caveats). But we benefit from considering the waters in which we swim and how they shape our sense of identity.

IF YOU'RE A FISH, THEN BE A FISH

A recording of the song "Big-Eyed Fish" first surfaced as part of the leaked *Lillywhite Sessions*, and eventually was polished and re-recorded for 2002's *Busted Stuff*. Beginning with an ascending series of notes picked on violin, the song eventually expands into the full band as Matthews sings a series of stories about various creatures who attempt to be something else: a fish tries to walk on land, a monkey tries to get a human job, a man tries to hold his breath. Each of these brief accounts end in tragedy, as they are unable to do something other than what they're meant to do.

At one point in the song, Matthews muses on how we sometimes imagine what it could be like to be something else. We may often romanticize who others are and wish we had their lives instead of our own. On occasion we may even try to obtain something close to what we see others have. Maybe this works every so often, but how much more is it usually the case that we fail due to unforeseen consequences, or we realize something about the reality of what a different lifestyle or identity entails? From far away, being a different person seems wonderful. Up close is a different story.

Thomas Merton wrote about the tension that each of us feel between our true selves and our false selves. The way he puts it, the best way one can give glory to God is to be who we are to our fullest capacity. A fish is at its best when being a fish. A monkey is honoring God best when being the best monkey it can be. So, too, does an individual human honor God, but also themselves, by living up to the best essence of themselves as possible.[5]

When striving to answer the question of who we are, this includes not only our history but what makes up our identity now: our intellectual gifts, our creative talents, what brings us joy, what makes us sad, what injustices make us angry, how we share ourselves with others, and how and who we love. From the perspective of both "Big-Eyed Fish" and Merton, living all of that as truly and as completely and as passionately as you can is who you are meant to be.

This isn't often easy, because we are also often tempted to present a false self to the world around us. We may not aspire to live someone else's life, but we may face pressure to do so from the culture that formed or that continues to form us. We may still feel a subconscious need to obtain acceptance from someone in our family of origin, so we behave a certain way. We may still harbor criticism or abuse from someone in our past that causes us to react to certain situations with fear or anxiety, or by closing ourselves

---

5. Merton, *New Seeds*, 29–30.

off. We may present ourselves as something we're not to receive accolades, inclusion, or love.

Our false self can be damaging for several reasons. First, it causes us to neglect or hide who we truly want to be. We are like a fish trying to walk on dry land, unaware that we are suffocating. We let our own gifts and interests fall by the wayside because we've deemed somebody else's expectations or judgment more important than those that we have for ourselves. In giving so much of our energy to being what others want, we end up living someone else's life rather than our own.

Investing in our false selves also denies the world the gifts we are able to offer it. How much more enriched would those around us be if we spoke with our own voice, sang our own song, stood up for what stokes our inner fire? What if we dared to be our own best selves over and against others' desire for everyone to follow a standard pattern of behavior and speech? How many others hiding behind their own false selves could be inspired to shed their plastic exteriors if they saw another person doing it first?

The question posed at the center of "Dancing Nancies" wonders if we could be anyone other than who we are. We may wish that things in our past had gone a different way; we may wonder what it could have been like for us if we were raised in a culture other than the one we had. But an equally important question is "Who are you now?" That is not to ask how you may better be the false self that others want you to present, but instead how you may, perhaps for the first time, be the authentic and true self you always have been.

Not only do you need it, but the world needs it as well.

9

THE CENTRALITY OF HUMAN COMMUNITY

"Funny The Way It Is" was the first single released from *Big Whiskey & the GrooGrux King*, which came out in 2009. The song explores ways that different situations might seem good for one person, but for someone else it would produce difficulty. A child in a war-torn area like Syria fears for his life every day, while more privileged and safe children in an American suburb might gleefully chase each other around with plastic guns. One person gives up on their educational dreams, while someone in poverty makes it a point to walk to their classes every day. One person is experiencing a nice quiet day relaxing on a lawn, while someone else is having the worst day of their life as first responders race to stop a fire in their home.

This song points out the various ways our situations are at times intertwined with others; at other times diametrically opposed to another's experience. All of this depends on where we're standing, where we've come from, what opportunities we've had or we'd like to have, and what benefit of the doubt we've been given due to our status or financial ability or race.

It truly is funny—or perhaps better descriptors might be "disturbing," "alarming," or "thought-provoking"—how these sorts of concurrent experiences and realities can happen, where one's own perspective or good fortune depends on how one views even the same event. How often do we consider the sirens in the distance while we sit on our porch enjoying a cold drink? What has happened in the life of one person able to eat fast food, while another can barely afford a daily meal? Two people can have such radically different experiences on the same day and may place different values on those experiences depending on where they're standing or whether they're able to relate.

While people who are well-off complain about some small inconvenience like a long wait for coffee or the cable going out, someone else is struggling to buy diapers for their newborn or trying to figure out how to pay for both rent and groceries. One person works long hours in a six-figure position, while another is still scraping by despite bouncing back and forth between two jobs seven days a week. We don't often consider what people in other parts of the world, let alone our own communities or even our own neighborhood, might be going through. We may not often consider how some may wish for certain comforts that we take for granted or possibilities that are open to us, nor how another might benefit from something we can offer them.

Some of this inability to perceive such things may be due to our not wanting to venture out of our comfort zones; another part of it may be our being so caught up in our own concerns that we don't have time to give to what someone else needs.

At times such experiences might be peripheral. Two people passing one another on the street might not give the other's situation much thought as they each rush to fulfill their obligations for the day. We may be oblivious to the worries of most others around us, in part because we might prefer things that way, but also because we either don't think to ask or are too embarrassed to share. What could we possibly do for someone else, anyway? What even momentary or miniscule difference would our intertwining predicaments produce?

"Funny The Way It Is" raises the question of what could happen if we just stopped to understand. While you may be sitting at home or at a coffeehouse reading this book, what is someone across the street worried or despairing or angry about? Or in those moments when you are wide awake at three in the morning concerned about what challenges the new day will bring, how much of a difference could it make to just have someone else know what you're upset about?

Due to our increased isolation from one another thanks to busy schedules and the beckoning glowing screens of our many technological devices, we are in danger of losing our sense of connection to one another; the relative nature of our lives, and the potential that a change in recognition and increased awareness could bring.

WHAT THE WIDOW GAVE

Jesus could have written his own version of "Funny The Way It Is," although he didn't find much funny about what was happening in his local synagogue:

> As he taught, he said, "Beware of the scribes, who like to walk around in long robes, and to be greeted with respect in the marketplaces, [39]and to have the best seats in the synagogues and places of honor at banquets! [40]They devour widows' houses and for the sake of appearance say long prayers. They will receive the greater condemnation."
> [41]He sat down opposite the treasury, and watched the crowd putting money into the treasury. Many rich people put in large sums. [42]A poor widow came and put in two small copper coins, which are worth a penny. [43]Then he called his disciples and said to them, "Truly I tell you, this poor widow has put in more than all those who are contributing to the treasury. [44]For all of them have contributed out of their abundance; but she out of her poverty has put in everything she had, all she had to live on." (Mark 12:38–44)

The scribes that Jesus mentions at the beginning of this episode would have been translators and interpreters of the Hebrew Torah for the people. They would have been granted authority and special status, and Jesus is calling out abuses of that power. He warns the people to beware of how this group receives such special accolades, because they may come at others' expense. From Jesus' perspective, these leaders like to be revered in public places and take the best seats at public gatherings and celebrations. But most egregiously, they take advantage of the poor. Jesus calls out their "devouring of widows' houses;" their exploitation of people's meager means.

Jesus' basic criticism is that these figures like being honorable religious people, but they don't really honor what their religion is about. They should seek to be servants rather than acting like they're above it all. They should seek to care for widows rather than take all they can from them. His words are for all who dress the part and say the right words, but act in very different ways. As discussed in chapter 5, they claim the branding of their tradition, but aren't much for pursuing its ethics.

As Jesus and the disciples sit across from the treasury, he observes an object lesson to illustrate his point play out in real time. First, they watch as wealthy people step up with large amounts to contribute. According to the law, this would have been a certain percentage of what they'd earned. So, in that sense, they are faithful. Jesus doesn't really have anything to criticize them for. He was, after all, Jewish himself, so he would have understood that they were following through on what they were commanded to do.

But then a widow—a flesh and blood example of one having her house devoured—enters, and she puts in two copper coins, which would have added up to about a penny. And this is where Jesus becomes more animated, as he suggests that she has put in much more than the wealthier attendees before her. She's not giving a percentage, because she doesn't have a percentage to give. She's just giving what she has.

Funny the way it is, Jesus observes, that one person's spare change (their "drop in the bucket," as it were) is another person's entire livelihood. And funny the way it is that this widow's offering will profit the very same ones who devour widow's houses. It's happening right in front of them, in this moment. Funny the way it is . . . except it isn't.

The different perspectives between the scribes and the widow, and later the wealthy contributors and the widow, are worth consideration. Funny the way it is, Jesus points out, that the ones purporting to serve God are denying God by taking from the widow, whom God repeatedly commands people to care for.

Recognizing such interrelated experiences and how one influences the other helps build awareness of how our own actions may impact others. Such recognition invites further awareness of what others are experiencing so that we may give kindness and aid more generously and responsibly. It invites us to be aware of our own sense of calling to use our resources and gifts to help others; to give out of our abundance so others may have something to begin with. It invites a sense of greater connectedness, where we are not our own but a part of something larger, and that kindness will have a positive ripple effect, just as exploitation or selfishness will have a negative one.

Let's say one final thing about the scribes and the widow: Jesus has concern for both. He wants the scribe to stop trying to be God, and instead to see God in the widow. The widow is dependent on the scribe for basic living; the scribe is dependent on her for opportunities to learn humility and exercise faithfulness. Both are connected to each other, and that connection may deepen through sharing what a common experience is like from different angles.

WHAT KEEPS US DIVIDED

"Cry Freedom" is the tenth track on the band's second major release *Crash*. It is a slower, more reflective song mostly driven by a few gentle chords strummed on guitar, although it eventually builds to a full band sound featuring a soaring violin part played by Boyd Tinsley. Dave Matthews has stated that inspiration from the song came from time spent in South Africa, and his observations around the fall of apartheid. One of the most notable events for Matthews that led to the song's composition was the murder of anti-apartheid leader Steve Biko.[1] The violence that striving for equality brings in response is difficult to watch, no matter its form.

The bulk of the song is a sharing of a dream for people to realize how connected we are; how we share much more in common than we realize. Many choose not to see this due to the artificial or emotional walls we erect between ourselves and others to ensure our own sense of isolation or safety. Matthews laments how we keep our own fellow world citizens from enjoying freedom by placing wealth-based or fear-based boundaries between ourselves and others, emphasizing our differences in class or race or creed as reasons to remain separated.

But what if we didn't? What if, Matthews asks, we stopped keeping ourselves from each other? What greater sense of community could we make possible through realizing our common needs and dreams and hopes? Could a shared cry for freedom ever overcome our differences?

In late January of 2017, the United States government issued a ban on travel for citizens of seven Middle Eastern countries: Iraq, Syria, Iran, Libya, Somalia, Sudan, and Yemen. This action immediately left travelers stranded in airports, and uncertain about their ability to be welcomed into the country that they hoped to enter for basic reasons such as work, education, or family. In addition, refugees seeking national shelter from the violence of their home country were denied access or were turned away. The reasoning given for this action had to do with security, but it left thousands of people suddenly without a home and without hope.

The reaction to this was immediate. Protests swelled at airports as people—American citizens—cited their country's responsibility to help those from other places, particularly when they were seeking refuge from regions made desolate by endless conflict. They proclaimed their support for welcoming people without regard for religious or ethnic background, because a country with

1. Martell, *Music for the People*, 62.

such vast resources and high stated values had a moral obligation to do so.

As I watched coverage of these protests myself, I was most struck by a homemade banner some had hung from a balcony that read in big black letters: "We will love and protect each other." It was a statement of defiance, but also one of support and of hope; a cry of freedom for all people despite differences, and that love can be stronger than fear. Those who hung this banner, along with thousands of others, chose to recognize what connects us rather than what divides us.

This was the dream of "Cry Freedom" made real. It was a momentary realization of what many have a longing for, and a sign that such a dream is possible. Such dreams do not materialize without struggle and they often need to be revisited to keep concrete expressions of authentic human community from fading, but they can and do happen.

The Teacher in the Biblical book of Ecclesiastes, whom we met in a previous chapter, shares his observations on what may happen to people who isolate themselves from each other:

> Again, I saw vanity under the sun: [8]the case of solitary individuals, without sons or brothers; yet there is no end to all their toil, and their eyes are never satisfied with riches. "For whom am I toiling," they ask, "and depriving myself of pleasure?" This also is vanity and an unhappy business. [9]Two are better than one, because they have a good reward for their toil. [10]For if they fall, one will lift up the other; but woe to one who is alone and falls and does not have another to help. [11]Again, if two lie together, they keep warm; but how can one keep warm alone? [12]And though one might prevail against another, two will withstand one. A threefold cord is not quickly broken. (Eccl 4:7–12)

In the first few lines, the Teacher sees people work daily and without much of a break, accumulating wealth and resources for themselves. He focuses on the people without loved ones who are only gaining such riches for their own enjoyment. Maybe this makes them happy for a while, but eventually they ask, who am I doing this for? Who will benefit from this besides the worker? What purpose might this serve for anyone else?

For some, maybe the answer doesn't matter. Like the narrator of "Too Much," they will fill their own accounts and stomachs as much as they can, and someone else can fight over it after they die. But from the Teacher's perspective, others experience a deep and profound loneliness when they realize they have nobody to help, nobody to rely on, nobody to share an abundant life with.

From there, the Teacher observes that people are stronger when they are together. One catches the other when either falls; each provides warmth for the other when lying together in bed. And when one needs additional support in a conflict, two will be stronger against one.

As connected as we think we are through innovations in technology and communication and information sharing and social media, we may be as disconnected as ever. We might be sitting right next to other people, yet each of us may be consumed by our own desires, our own devices, our own concerns. We may even have ways of convincing ourselves that we are better off relying on ourselves to solve our own problems, whether out of pride or embarrassment or fear of rejection. And some may choose to believe that, as they work for themselves, so is their resulting wealth only for their own use.

But the question the Teacher hears is still with us: who are you working for? For whom are you toiling, if one eats while another starves, one enjoys abundance while another struggles in scarcity, one rests in unearned privilege while another faces undeserved prejudice, one devours widows' houses while another widow gives all she has?

Our human connection rises us above the divides that we place between ourselves and other people. Who could we help stand again after they fall, or who will help us when one bad day upends all that we thought made us secure?

"Funny The Way It Is" observes that we are more connected than we think; that our views of the world can inform each other's experiences if we take time to consider how it is so. The question and the dream behind "Cry Freedom" is an active breaking-down of the ways we keep each other from such consideration, and a recognition of our mutual dependence for well-being and peace; that generous sharing and reaching out to understand and assist our local and global neighbor lifts all of us higher.

We will love and protect each other. Making that our common hope and dream may bring greater freedom to all.

10

THE CALL
TO TAKE ACTION

The song "Everyday" has an interesting history, as well as a certain polarizing place among Dave Matthews Band's fanbase. Its origins are rooted in a very early song in the band's catalogue, simply titled "#36," which itself has a notable beginning. The chorus of the latter song repeats the name of Chris Hani, a South African anti-apartheid activist who was tragically killed. Matthews conceived the song originally as a tribute to him, but the lyrics evolved over time to have a more romantic feel. This inspiration itself reveals the band's awareness and desire to speak out about causes that they're passionate about.

A musical arrangement similar to "#36" serves as the foundation for "Everyday," the third single and the final track on the band's album of same name, released in 2001. The two resemble each other so closely, in fact, that people see the latter evolving from the former. When the band plays "Everyday" in concert, the crowd tends to sing the refrain from "#36" during interludes, and the band often segues into the latter song by the end.

"Everyday" is a positive, upbeat song, focusing on the need for people to show compassion for each other, which sometimes might involve getting down in the messiness of another person's problems to help them. The tone of the chorus sounds joyful, but also has a certain pleading quality to it as a call to not only recognize our dependence on and connection to each other, but to act on it.

The video for "Everyday" was released several months after September 11th, 2001. It features a man waking up and going through a typical morning routine of getting dressed and brushing his teeth before wandering the streets of busy city areas trying to engage strangers on the sidewalk. At first, nobody responds to whatever he's saying, leaving the viewer to wonder what he's trying to do. Eventually, one person stops, listens to his brief pitch, and goes in for a hug. The rest of the video builds on this positive response, with him hugging more and more people, eventually including a few celebrities and members of the band.

The video is simple in concept, and poignant and uplifting given the time it was released. But the implications of both the song and the video offer cause for reflection: how many would consider walking the streets of their own town offering hugs to strangers? What kinds of risks would this simple attempt at kindness bring? What kinds of fears might even the thought of engaging in this small gesture raise?

The critique of religion at the heart of many Dave Matthews Band songs, as well as many interviews that Matthews gives when belief is a subject, is that faith is often used for a sense of personal comfort or as a tool to justify oppressive actions. But as has been discussed, any form of faith that holds up virtues like kindness, love, peacemaking, and reconciliation should result in its adherents living them out in concrete ways.

This is why Matthews can express admiration for Jesus: because he often proclaimed and embodied such values as part of his life and ministry. But sometimes those same values get lost in translation between the master and the disciple. It is much easier to make figures like Jesus or Gandhi or Martin Luther King Jr. into mythical heroes to honor from afar or express admiration for without seriously delving into the ways they pushed the systemic status quo, criticized those who didn't show compassionate regard for the most vulnerable, and required some form of sacrificial transformation in outlook and behavior from purported followers.

This is the difference between faith-as-creed and faith-as-trust; between serious consideration of how belief is meant to influence action, because action is how change happens. And such change often involves some form of discomfort or risk, even in something as small as walking up to strangers and asking if they'd like a hug. But what kind of a difference could a hug make in the trajectory of somebody's day?

BEYOND BELIEF

"Gaucho" is the fourth track on the band's album *Away From the World*, released in 2012. The song offers a brief overview of human evolution, from the earliest days of making tools and weapons from sticks and rocks to its more advanced accomplishments like traveling to space. But the song also observes that with all the possibilities we've uncovered for exploration and discovery have also come more sophisticated ways of hurting each other. While the song asks whether we can endure as a species with such potential for our own destruction, it also calls people to do more than just have faith that things can be different. The only way things will get better in any observable way is if people translate their belief into something more.

This same sentiment is expressed in a small letter toward the end of the New Testament called James, named after the purported writer who also was the head of the early church in Jerusalem and thought to be the brother of Jesus. In the second chapter of this letter, the author notes that if belief is to have any impact on the world, it needs to lead to something:

> What good is it, my brothers and sisters, if you say you have faith but do not have works? Can faith save you? [15]If a brother or sister is naked and lacks daily food, [16]and one of you says to them, "Go in peace; keep warm and eat your fill," and yet you do not supply their bodily needs,

what is the good of that? ¹⁷So faith by itself, if it has no works, is dead. ¹⁸But someone will say, "You have faith and I have works." Show me your faith apart from your works, and I by my works will show you my faith. ¹⁹You believe that God is one; you do well. Even the demons believe—and shudder. ²⁰Do you want to be shown, you senseless person, that faith apart from works is barren? ²¹Was not our ancestor Abraham justified by works when he offered his son Isaac on the altar? ²²You see that faith was active along with his works, and faith was brought to completion by the works. ²³Thus the scripture was fulfilled that says, "Abraham believed God, and it was reckoned to him as righteousness," and he was called the friend of God. ²⁴You see that a person is justified by works and not by faith alone. ²⁵Likewise, was not Rahab the prostitute also justified by works when she welcomed the messengers and sent them out by another road? ²⁶For just as the body without the spirit is dead, so faith without out works is also dead. (Jas 2:14–26)

For James, to have one's own theological ducks in a row might cause them to feel good. And some may even see the primary purpose of faith-as-creed as feeling secure and safe in one's own correctness. But what good is that to the hungry person who needs food, the person freezing in the cold with no jacket, the lonely person with nobody to offer support or access to care?

The writer of James declares that faith is not enough; that it should first lead to some form of transformation for the believer, which in turn will lead to the lives of others changing even in some small way through their actions. This is the essence of faith-as-trust in action: moving from keeping a list of what one thinks are the right beliefs in one's head to trusting in their truth by serving and helping others.

The challenge that James offers comes in verse 18: "show me your faith apart from your works." That is, show me what kind of a difference your faith makes for you or for the world in general if it doesn't move or inspire you to do anything. Alternatively, he continues, "I by my works will show you my faith." That is, actions such as helping people meet their needs, reaching out in care and concern, and speaking up about issues related to peace and justice will reveal the effectiveness of one's faith; whether it has truly been inspiring and life-changing in the heart and mind of the person professing it.

I once attended a national meeting of my denomination, the United Church of Christ, as a delegate to participate in their official business agenda. This role involved starting my day bright and early with a continental breakfast and a briefing on what the day might hold for us as representatives to this gathering.

If you aren't familiar with the UCC, the national setting of our church often takes public stands on a variety of justice issues such as speaking out against racism and discrimination, advocating for the poor, promoting gender equality, supporting workers' rights, and so on. Such stands and statements would be a part of this national meeting, as they often are.

The walk from our delegate meeting at the hotel to the convention center involved passing through the downtown area of a large city, and it always featured interactions with homeless individuals asking for a meal or a small handout to get them through the day. Many of us, as either experience has taught or reflexive human nature causes, tended to pass right by or mumble some excuse about not having anything to give. And, of course, this was while on our way to a day's worth of speeches and proclamations and sermons and prayers about helping those most in need.

For a few of us, this disconnect was upsetting and convicting. That first day we thought about what we might be able to do to reconcile what we were spending this meeting talking about with the needs of the people just outside the convention center's doors.

The next morning during our delegate meeting, we finally came up with a plan: we gathered up all the leftover fruit and bagels from the breakfast, stuffed them in our backpacks, and during our morning walk offered them to passers-by or to those asking us for help. Much like the main character in the "Everyday" video, not everyone was receptive. Even some of our fellow delegates steered clear of what we were doing, viewing our effort with some degree of suspicion or hesitancy. Our attempt wasn't perfect in execution, but it's what we thought of to try changing belief to action; transforming the faith-as-creed we'd been hearing during this church gathering into faith-as-trust.

Humanity can be quite creative in the ways we do harm to one another, and as "Gaucho" observes, our methods of doing so have evolved and brought potential for greater and more destructive consequences. More than faith-as-creed will be needed to turn any of it around; to give hope to the despairing, to challenge the intentions and implications of policies that demean and dehumanize, to offer any show of support or encouragement or protection to those victimized by the oppression of individuals or systems.

Maybe a hug or a bagel doesn't seem like much, but it could lead to more for both the one offering them and in the one receiving them. For the one offering them, it can lead to further seeking out how to help others and to cultivating new habits that result in further acts of love. For the recipient, it can lead to greater self-worth, a sense that they're not alone in their struggle, a renewed hope that humanity is capable of goodness.

Belief carries with it the potential for all of this, but only when acted upon beyond thoughts, words, sermons, and prayers. Reaching out via faith-as-trust will show that faith-as-creed has made a difference. By working on behalf of others through even the subtlest gestures and smallest risks, belief is made real, and may lead to greater gestures and risks over time. And if an entire group or neighborhood or community moves beyond belief to action, it could lead to quite a lot of change.

WHERE FAITH AND HUMAN
CONNECTION LEAD

The previous chapter included a discussion based on the song "Funny The Way It Is," pointing out the ways our experiences are either interrelated or could be seen differently depending on our background or life circumstances. We are more connected than we often realize, and our greater awareness of how our actions may impact others or how others may understand that the same event can lead to more careful consideration of our ability to help others, a greater appreciation for our own resources or opportunities, and more consideration of our interdependence with those around us.

Like faith, such awareness should lead to action if it has truly taken root within us. When we truly allow to affect us the suffering, injustice, and scarcity that others are forced to live with, we may be led to ask how we may respond as fellow members of the greater human community.

In all honesty, such awareness and questioning can weigh heavily and be quite daunting. After all, with so much need of addressing and healing and engagement, we may become so overwhelmed by it all that offering aid in some small way may bring confusion, heartbreak, despair, and the temptation to give up before one even begins. Where does one start? And could anything I do really make any kind of a difference?

We've discussed those uncertainties already, where even hugs and offering pieces of fruit to someone can be the start of something bigger for all involved. But some theological and spiritual circles tend to downplay faith that results in works or recognizing our connection to others in need. So strong is the emphasis in faith-as-creed among some believers that any call to action is met with one of several responses.

First, some may share the thought already expressed, that small acts don't matter because their impact won't last in any meaningful way. We may be called to show love and concern for others, but don't expect it to matter as much as winning someone over to the right way of belief. This view tends to prefer argument over action, where conversion is the primary goal rather than meeting any physical or emotional needs from which one is suffering. This view is soundly addressed by the James passage quoted earlier: faith includes concern for the hungry, rather than ignoring hunger at the expense of correct belief. After all, if belief is truly correct, it will take such hunger seriously and be demonstrated through such concern.

Second and closely related to the first is the view that the next life is more important than the current one. This view states that the needs we experience in this life are temporary compared to the greater concern of where you may spend the next. This view also tends to carry with it the idea that this world will eventually end anyway, so spending any time or energy trying to improve it for others will be futile on a long-enough timeline.

Such approaches to the relationship between faith and action are both defeatist and insensitive, not to mention the antithesis of what examples from Jesus, the prophets, and James discussed in previous chapters call people of faith to be concerned about and to do on behalf of others. These views often add to people's burdens rather than ease them, not to mention adding to the long track record of hurt, suspicion, and rejection of Christian belief to which they often lead.

People of faith are not called to isolation, nor are they called to expressions of belief that only address spiritual concerns. A healthy spirituality will encompass all of life, including its physical, mental, and emotional aspects, impacting them for the better. If one tries to divorce the former from the rest, it ignores what spirituality is really meant to transform for the better.

The song "Raven" is the sixth track on *Busted Stuff*. The first version that appeared on *The Lillywhite Sessions* has different lyrics that reflect on the futility of existence. When it was re-recorded for *Busted Stuff*, it came with new words, though with no less of a bleak outlook.

The song depicts a conversation between a father and son, where the son is pondering a portable version of the world that he's holding in his hand. The father admonishes him to be careful with it, since there aren't any others. The boy responds dryly that it will take his entire life to reverse all the harmful things that the father's generation did to it.

If we take the story of this song beyond what the lyrics share and envision the extent of the boy's work as he grows older, its practical side becomes complex. Not only might he and the rest of his generation have to work endlessly to improve the world so much, but they'd have to do so while dealing with pushback from people who like things the way they are or who benefit personally from its current state, no matter how damaging it is for others. He would need to spend a substantial amount of his time convincing others that the changes he wants to make are worth making. He'll need to make the case that not only will they enjoy the improvements that he proposes, but when the boy is his father's age having a similar conversation with his own son, the back-and-forth might be different.

To consider the implications that one's faith is meant to have on the world is to consider our connection to one another; how our decisions are intertwined with and have an effect not only on those around us, but on those who will inherit this world after us. To claim no responsibility, or to minimize the impact even one person could have, is to discount the calling that faith involves as well as ignore those connections that span beyond present concerns to generations who will come after us.

Faith-as-creed calls its adherents to more. Faith-as-trust moves forward despite not knowing what could result. Even the smallest token, or enough small tokens offered in tandem, could begin to make a much bigger difference than we'll ever know.

11

DEATH AND GRIEF

Included on Dave Matthews's solo album, *Some Devil*, is a song called "Gravedigger." In it, he provides snapshots of several lives, including the years they were born and died, as well as some snippet of who they were while they lived. This series of stories conveys the image that we are walking through a cemetery reading tombstones and remembering something of each resident. In the opening verse, for instance, Matthews walks past the grave of a woman whose sons were killed in World War II. He reflects on what that experience might have been like for her before moving on to the next marker.

The song provides a reflection on the rich stories that any graveyard contains and that the people buried there can no longer tell. If any of them have loved ones who still visit or remember them, they can help fill in the gaps through their own memories, but otherwise there are just rows of marble as final testaments.

In the chorus, Matthews entreats the title character to do something for him, hoping that he won't make his grave the standard depth. This brief request is an acknowledgement of death's inevitable nature. The key word in this part of the song is "when." That is, when the time comes—as it will for all of us—please prepare my final resting place so I still can feel life happening above me. The singer is accepting and even embracing his eventual death, rather than attempting to run away from it.

When asked why he seems to write about death so much in his music, Matthews has reiterated the importance of now, addressed in an earlier chapter. For him, death should be a more widely-addressed subject because it has such grand implications for how we live. To place all our hope in an afterlife while ignoring this one is, to him, a way to avoid what's right in front of us.[1]

These thoughts echo the sentiments expressed in "Gravedigger." In both, Matthews is not running from death, but neither is he running toward it, attempting to hasten its approach. Nor is this a nihilism stating that nothing in this life matters because we're all going to die someday, as our earlier consideration of "Tripping Billies" showed.

Instead, a song like "Gravedigger" merely acknowledges that death is one of the few known and unavoidable things that everyone faces at some point. Because of this, Matthews says, it gives life an urgency rather than a pointlessness. If the gravedigger will one day prepare a rectangular bed for us, we'd better make the most of things before he does.

Included also in Matthews's answer, however, is a critique of a spirituality of death that often threatens to cheapen not only life's final chapter, but the way we approach everything that comes before it. A preoccupation with what might happen in the afterlife, according to Matthews, causes people to avoid hardships that we encounter in this life that we could learn from, as well as enjoy its pleasures as fully and completely as we are meant to do.

To shift one's focus from where our souls end up in the next life to what our souls are experiencing in this one may seem like a radical idea for some, depending on one's religious background or upbringing. Many Christian traditions stress a concern for one's destination after our bodies give out, as well as bringing as many others along with us as we can. The implication for many of these same theological strands is a mission to prevent as many people as possible from an eternity of damnation.

1. Scaggs, "Devil in Dave Matthews," para. 42.

The result of such a strong focus on the afterlife is that one's entire reason for living becomes preparing for what happens after death. Such a view can become a handy excuse for avoiding the many real ways people suffer in this life through violence, hunger, disease, poverty, discrimination, oppression, disaster, and environmental degradation. If one believes that this life doesn't matter nearly as much as the next, it's easy to ignore the deep and lasting effects that these and many other forms of tragedy affect the quality of life of millions of people every day, including those in our own communities or families, or even ourselves.

For Matthews, it shouldn't be that easy. To face death seriously is to face life seriously, good and bad.

EMBRACING LIFE'S SEASONS

The Teacher from Ecclesiastes wrestles with the point of existence and what brings true and lasting joy. A passage from chapter 3 may be the most well-known, even if many haven't sat down to read it:

> For everything there is a season, and a time for every matter under heaven: [2]a time to be born, and a time to die; a time to plant, and a time to pluck up what is planted; [3]a time to kill, and a time to heal; a time to break down, and a time to build up; [4]a time to weep, and a time to laugh; a time to mourn, and a time to dance; [5]a time to throw away stones, and a time to gather stones together; a time to embrace, and a time to refrain from embracing; [6]a time to seek, and a time to lose; a time to keep, and a time to throw away; [7]a time to tear, and a time to sew; a time to keep silence, and a time to speak; [8]a time to love, and a time to hate; a time for war, and a time for peace. [9]What gain have the workers from their toil? [10]I have seen the business that God has given to everyone to be busy with.
>
> [11]He has made everything suitable for its time; moreover he has put a sense of past and future into their minds, yet they cannot find out what God has done from the beginning to the end. [12]I know that there is nothing

better for them than to be happy and enjoy themselves as long as they live; [13]moreover, it is God's gift that all should eat and drink and take pleasure in all their toil. [14]I know that whatever God does endures forever; nothing can be added to it, nor anything taken from it; God has done this, so that all should stand in awe before him. [15]That which is, already has been; that which is to be, already is; and God seeks out what has gone by. (Eccl 3:1–15)

The first part of this passage observes that life seasons come and go, and each invite or require actions that seem appropriate and necessary. There are times to till the soil for something new to grow, and there are times to pluck up what has grown or that is no longer needed. There are times to express joy through dance or song, and there are times to spend in grief, either alone or with others. There are times to let something go and times to preserve something else.

At the very beginning of this passage, the Teacher makes the two largest and most truthful claims: there is a time to live, and then there is a time to die. There is a season where we may indulge in all of life's gifts, savoring them and sharing them with loved ones, and then that final season of our lives comes when it is time to lay things down and await what comes after our last breath.

The Teacher does not dwell on this fact with any kind of morbid celebration or fascination. He just notes that some things pass and other things take their place, and that includes human lives, one generation to the next. "Gravedigger" anticipates this, as Matthews asks the title character to give certain attentions to his body once life has left it.

And yet, much like Matthews does in his explanation of why he writes about death so much, the Teacher sees that everything that comes before this final season carries an added importance. All the times that come before that last time of dying have a certain urgency; that there is nothing better for people "than to be happy and enjoy themselves as long as they live" (Eccl 3:12). In fact, from his perspective, it is "God's gift" that people do this.

As a pastor, a single week for me can involve an incredible fluctuation in being with people who are in one season of life to those in one far different. On a Saturday, I might officiate a wedding between two people barely into their twenties, anticipating the beginning of careers and not yet ready to start a family. On a Tuesday I might visit the bedside of a sixty-year-old man recovering from heart surgery who admits he'll need to cut back on his love of salty foods from now on. On a Thursday, I might oversee the funeral of a beloved wife, mother, and grandmother who lived into a ripe old age, and later that afternoon visit a couple in their eighties, the husband of which is in the middle stages of dementia. And the following Sunday, I'll interact with a group of elementary-age kids as they bounce around eating donuts and sipping juice.

There is a time for each of these, whether the exuberance of youth, the carefulness of middle age, and the anticipatory grief of late life. Each brings its own causes for thankfulness and its own concerns. We may favor some seasons over others, but we may sit with the question of how to maximize the quality of each, both for ourselves and others.

As we've already explored, the observations both of the Teacher and of Matthews's songs are not an invitation to indulgence at the expense of responsibility, but a recognition that as times come and go, each of them should be treated as a precious gift rather than a wasted opportunity.

One cannot do this if one is always placing hope in the life to come at the expense of the life that is. That time will come, but the times before that are to be savored just as much. Matthews has acknowledged how often he seems to write about death, seizing the day, and enjoying the present moment. But the fact of death for him helps create this urgency; this idea that death gives us fewer causes to take this life for granted and become too focused on life's little irritations.[2]

---

2. Mason, "Dave Matthews Band," para. 55.

HOPE DURING GRIEF

Even if a spirituality of death should include the implication that all of life before that final season is a gift, how might it also take seriously the fear and grief that death causes? Even if death has inspired us not to avoid living but rather to embrace it, what hope or reassurance might we find in or after its approach?

The band seemed to have these sorts of questions on its mind when they entered the studio to finish *Big Whiskey & the GrooGrux King*, soon after the death of founding member LeRoi Moore. With Moore having already contributed to several completed songs and with many other recorded improvisations of his available, the band made a conscious choice to feature their departed friend and bandmate as much as possible. Violinist Boyd Tinsley once described how they carried their grief with them into these sessions, and how the first realization that Moore wasn't in the booth listening while he was playing caused him to break down.[3]

The inspiration for the album's name comes from a nickname the band had for Moore, "Grux," and the first song (by the same name) is one such improvised saxophone solo. The nickname is invoked numerous times later on the album on the song "Why I Am," which features some of the most overt references to the group's love for and missing of Moore.

The overall mood of the song is upbeat, driving, and defiant. The verses are a whirlwind of imagery, with each line carrying a forcefulness that accompanies the music well. The bridge echoes the Ecclesiastes passage referenced earlier, as it bluntly states that we all have the same exit eventually, and there's no avoiding it.

Just as the Teacher reflects on life presenting different seasons and times for everything, so here the band sings of the world containing successes and failures, wrongs and rights, and relationships that gel or clash. And no matter what quantities of each the world presents during one's lifetime, the fact remains that death is the only way out. After these general sentiments about the frantic nature of life and its many seasons, and because one particular

---

3. Mason, "Dave Matthews Band," para. 50.

death was still heavy on the minds of the band, it speaks of a longing to be back with the "GrooGrux King."

As Matthews has sung several times in the song, he (and the rest of the band, by extension) is still in a mode of celebration, as if their friend was still around. They continue to honor who he was in life and to each of them as a friend and fellow musician. These lines seem to conjure the image of a perpetual wake, where every time Moore's friends are together enjoying whiskey just as before, they'll remember him.

This song does reference an afterlife, though Matthews's own beliefs about its existence or importance to how one lives show that it is not the primary driver of its inclusion. What he seems more interested in conveying is that no matter what comes after death, he wants to be with his friend. Whether that involves traditional images of eternal blessing or torment, or something else entirely, if he can be with the people he loves, it won't matter. Just their presence will make anything that happens more bearable, if not outright enjoyable.

RETURNING TO DUST

In the final verses to chapter 3, the Teacher's thoughts on life's seasons seem to take a darker turn:

> Moreover I saw under the sun that in the place of justice, wickedness was there, and in the place of righteousness, wickedness was there as well. [17]I said in my heart, God will judge the righteous and the wicked, for he has appointed a time for every matter, and for every work. [18]I said in my heart with regard to human beings that God is testing them to show that they are but animals. [19]For the fate of humans and the fate of animals is the same; as one dies, so dies the other. They all have the same breath, and humans have no advantage over the animals; for all is vanity. [20]All go to one place; all are from the dust, and all turn to dust again. [21]Who knows whether the human spirit goes upward and the spirit of animals goes downward to the earth? [22]So I saw that there is nothing better

than that all should enjoy their work, for that is their lot; who can bring them to see what will be after them? (Eccl 3:16–22)

Over the course of our lives, we face times of joy and times of pain, times of injustice and wickedness and times of equity and kindness. Life's highs and lows are each with us in variable measure, and those measures change over time. But the Teacher expresses some faith that God will deal with all of it, and the presence of both can have a humbling effect on helping us realize our limitations and fallacies, as well as our temporary place in the universe no matter how highly we like to think of ourselves.

Eventually, the Teacher observes, we return to dust. Like Matthews, he doesn't seem sure of what comes next. He even suggests that anyone who thinks they are certain don't know any better than the rest of us: "Who knows whether the human spirit goes upward and the spirit of animals goes downward to the earth" (verse 21)? Even as he is still working all of this out, he knows that enjoying this present gift of life is what we are meant to do in the meantime.

Certain forms of spirituality like to treat death as an enemy; as something to be avoided, fought, ignored, or beaten, no matter the cost. This includes certain forms of Christianity, which often minimizes human suffering and pain. Such strands are at the heart of Matthews's critique that he gives in the referenced interview, where he argues that there is a danger in placing so much of an emphasis on the afterlife that they end up not taking injurious or life-threatening circumstances as the serious situations that they are. War, poverty, disease, mental illness, discrimination based on race, gender, orientation, or ability receive a passing glance, a token prayer, a few dollars given to charity, or some well-intentioned-yet-unhelpful words, under the reasoning that this will be over soon and a better life is coming.

Christian spirituality does have resurrection as one of its central claims, and the hope of life eternal is part of what is preached at times of dying and at funerals. One may even quote Paul's words from 1 Corinthians: "Where, O death, is your victory? Where, O death, is your sting" (1 Corinthians 15:55)? Such a verse was written to reassure readers that something greater is possible due to what God first did through Jesus in raising him from the dead.

And yet before victory, the sting remains. That sting comes in the form of disaster or tragedy or cancer or violence or being unable to afford necessary care. The effects of this sting are acute to those who are forced to feel them every day. To those sitting in such pain, speaking solely of the afterlife at the expense of what could be done in the meantime to alleviate such suffering only compounds the problem. And it runs the risk of ignoring the real effects that pain and loss have on everyone involved.

A spirituality that embraces death; that sees it as another season of life for which there is a natural and proper time, carries several potential positive effects that assist us in placing it in its proper context.

Once a year, many Christians observe a day on the church calendar called Ash Wednesday. This day may occur any time between the beginning of February and the beginning of March, and is the first day of a period called Lent, which comes right before Easter. The central practice on Ash Wednesday is to allow someone—a clergy figure or otherwise—to place ashes on one's forehead in the shape of a cross, with accompanying words that vary on these: "Remember that you are dust, and to dust you shall return."

It may seem like a morbid practice to some, but it serves several purposes. First, it reminds people that they are mortal beings. We may invest in all the "anti-aging" cream we wish in attempts to deny this truth, but it remains that this life is a finite one, with every positive and negative implication that results from knowing that. We'll all be talking to the gravedigger sooner or later.

Second, this practice communicates something about our dependence on and need for care and sustenance beyond ourselves. For some, this may be God or some other transcendent. For others, it may be other people. For many, even if we've never thought about it in these terms, this may include those who make the medicine we need, those who administer care in any form, those who determine the financial viability of life's necessities, those who keep watch while we are asleep. We are not our own, and we do not exist only by what we can provide for ourselves, but instead we are dependent upon others for what we need to keep living.

Finally, this isn't usually mentioned during Ash Wednesday observances, but it is something that Matthews might add: before we return to dust, we have things to do. We have other people who are also dependent upon us. We have pleasures to enjoy, such as weekend getaways, our families, whiskey, or friends who support us but who might also push us to be better. Before our story ends, we have so much to wonder at and explore and love, and while we may have hope in what follows, we may find hope in what comes before as well.

A spirituality that takes death seriously does not have to be fatalistic. It does not have to dwell on the inevitable end that comes to every life, nor does it have to state that everybody should indulge in as much revelry as possible before our own time comes. The former misses out on what one's current season of life has to offer or what they may offer while in it; the latter falls into the common idea that our final season is to be avoided at all costs.

Rather, death invites a humility. It reminds us that we are mortal beings who are not in sole control. It reminds us that there is limited time to enrich others' lives, as well as our own. It reminds us that no amount of money or self-medicating indulgence will help us get around what is natural for everyone. It reminds us that the suffering of this life has real effects which will be concealed by casting all our attention to what comes after.

By taking death seriously, we may take life seriously. We're presented with times to love and times to laugh, as long as our story endures.

AFTERWORD

If you've read this far, you might have noticed how focused much of this book has been on what faith means for the present moment. Some may feel frustrated by that, because certain strands of Christianity place such a high emphasis on what happens after we die and where people may be destined to spend the afterlife. But the overall focus of Dave Matthews Band's music is on what this life has to offer: what brings joy, what helps others, and how well we can live as individuals and in community now. As stated at the beginning, I've intended to have the band's art lead the discussion, so such a focus is a natural result. But beyond that, people of faith could probably stand to take what they're meant to do in the here and now with more serious consideration.

As I've tried to show, I believe that the music of Dave Matthews Band presents certain views and themes that may inform or critique spirituality and faith, and in that sense has great value for those with an interest in exploring or deepening their own belief and practice. And an emphasis on how faith may inspire us to live and treat one another is one that goes back to most writers and figures of the Bible. We could probably use a few more reminders of how our own Scriptures, not to mention Jesus himself, intended for us to conduct ourselves in the name of God.

In this group's music, we hear pushback against some of the dangerous ways that people use religious devotion to rationalize hateful worldviews and carry out actions that serve certain political ends, but don't look much like what their faith's figurehead taught or modeled. We hear observations that faith as a set of beliefs doesn't hold much potential to be life- or world-altering without actions, and that those acts should have a certain character that reflects the best of what humanity is called to be: loving, peace-making, merciful, kind, and mindful of others. We hear an admiration for Jesus as an example of how to live out these ideals, not just a brand name to stamp on what we'd rather do. We hear strong encouragement to appreciate the gifts that life presents to us in any given moment, while being careful to watch for ways in which we become abusive of or overly dependent upon them. My hope is that the reader can see how all these ideas are consistent with a life of faith.

But if some are frustrated by how much this book focused on this one and only earthly life that we are given, others might have bristled at just how often quotes from the Bible made an appearance. These were to show that the writers of these texts had some of the same views and struggles that a popular band has been singing about for the past twenty-five years, and that the two are more compatible than believers, skeptics, and curious fans alike may realize.

Dave Matthews Band's songs are but one cultural entry point of many into faith's potential to give or restrict life. You may find such entry points through other favorite bands, books, movies, or TV shows. Each also will diverge in their own ways, but a consideration of their perspectives can offer new insight into the familiar, or a breath of fresh air for those weary of or bruised by traditions that they've been a part of.

If nothing else, I hope that you have seen how these reflections may enrich or redeem your own understanding of a faith you love or that you've left behind. I hope that this band's call to show love, receive each moment as a gift, and share such a gift with others have been the reaffirmation or challenge that you've been looking for or that you didn't know you needed.

I acknowledge that this book does not often give easy answers or present clear doctrinal statements. As discussed, this band's music doesn't always present neat and tidy scenarios, either. Rather, they describe experiences and provide a soundtrack for times of joy, sadness, uncertainty, anger, and doubt; all the typical situations we may encounter on any given day.

Religious belief also helps do this, as our own faith-as-creed and faith-as-trust may provide insight and encouragement and help name our times of struggle and happiness. And like music, spirituality is most meaningful when it provides a language for how to navigate our lives rather than a clear and absolute prescription for where it's all going. This way of approaching a life of faith admits uncertainty while also emphasizing our connection to something greater than ourselves. We may not possess a complete awareness of who we are or what life will bring next, but we may at least find some sense and solace in sacred words, expressive songs, and our relationship with others. And we may describe this complex web of connection as having a transcendent quality, even if we may call it by different names.

I've mentioned several times that Dave Matthews once said that he uses the term "God" to refer to everything he doesn't know. If we who identify as believers were a little more open to admit everything we don't know, maybe many of us would see God more regularly in each day we are given. And as a result, we'll treasure and use that gift well.

I'll keep hoping for that.

BIBLIOGRAPHY

Arnum, Eric. "Dave Matthews Explains Himself in 'Storytellers' Taping." http://www.mtv.com/news/513057/dave-matthews-explains-himself-in-storytellers-taping/.

Brueggemann, Walter. *The Message of the Psalms.* Minneapolis: Augsburg, 1984.

Chonin, Neva. "In the Studio with Dave Matthews." *Rolling Stone,* April 17, 2002. https://www.rollingstone.com/music/news/in-the-studio-with-dave-matthews-20020417.

Cooper, Betsy, et al. "Exodus: Why Americans are Leaving Religion—and Why They're Unlikely to Come Back." https://www.prri.org/research/prri-rns-poll-nones-atheist-leaving-religion/.

Delancey, Morgan. *Dave Matthews Band: Step Into the Light.* Toronto: ECW, 2001.

"Eh Hee." https://www.revolvy.com/main/index.php?s=Eh+Hee.

Erickson, Lori. "On a Busy Street Corner with Thomas Merton." *Spiritual Travels: Practical Advice for Soulful Journeys* (blog), n.d. https://www.spiritualtravels.info/ens-columns/on-a-busy-street-corner-with-thomas-merton/.

Graham, Tim. "Rock Star Dave Matthews on God: 'More Irritating Than Santa Claus.'" *NewsBusters* (blog), *Media Research Center,* November 16, 2007. https://www.newsbusters.org/blogs/nb/tim-graham/2007/11/16/rock-star-dave-matthews-god-more-irritating-santa-claus.

Gross, Stanley J. "Like Parent, Like Child: The Enduring Influence of Family." https://psychcentral.com/lib/like-parent-like-child-the-enduring-influence-of-family/.

Hamman, Jaco J. *Becoming a Pastor: Forming Self and Soul for Ministry.* Cleveland: Pilgrim, 2007.

Ivens, Michael. *Understanding the Spiritual Exercises.* Herefordshire, UK: Gracewing, 2008.

Kelly, Amy. "Stefan Lessard of the Dave Matthews Band: 'Every Show Is For LeRoi.'" https://www.ultimate-guitar.com/news/interviews/stefan_lessard_of_the_dave_matthews_band_every_show_is_for_leroi.html.

Bibliography

Martell, Nevin. *Music for the People: Dave Matthews Band*. New York: Pocket, 2004.

Mason, Anthony. "The Dave Matthews Band Opens Up." *CBS*, May 29, 2009. https://www.cbsnews.com/news/the-dave-matthews-band-opens-up/.

Maurer, Daniel D. *Endure: The Power of Spiritual Assets for Resilience to Trauma & Stress*. St. Paul: Mount Curve, 2017.

Merton, Thomas. *New Seeds of Contemplation*. New York: New Directions, 1972.

Meyer, Chris. "Phish, Dead & Company, and DMB Among Top 50 Grossing Tours of 2016." https://liveforlivemusic.com/news/phish-dead-company-dmb-among-top-50-grossing-tours-2016/.

Q on CBC. "Dave Matthews on Q TV." https://www.youtube.com/watch?v=fZbseUM1T_A.

Saint John of the Cross. *The Dark Night of the Soul*. New York: Barnes and Noble, 2005.

Scaggs, Austin. "The Devil In Dave Matthews." *Rolling Stone*, June 23, 2011. https://www.rollingstone.com/music/news/the-devil-in-dave-matthews-rolling-stones-2004-cover-story-20110623.

Serpick, Evan. "Dave Matthews Shares the Stories Behind 'Big Whiskey and the GrooGrux King.'" *Rolling Stone*, June 10, 2009. https://www.rollingstone.com/music/news/dave-matthews-shares-the-stories-behind-big-whiskey-and-the-groogrux-king-20090610.

Ulene, Valerie. "A Teen's Friends Are a Powerful Influence." *Los Angeles Times*, April 11, 2011. http://articles.latimes.com/2011/apr/11/health/la-he-the-md-teens-friends-20110411.

Van Noy, Nikki. *So Much to Say: Dave Matthews Band 20 Years on the Road*. New York: Simon & Schuster, 2011.

Vogel, Michael D. "Dave Matthews Band—Before These Crowded Streets: Finding The Groove With Dave Matthews." http://www.vogelism.com/book/dave-matthews-band-before-these-crowded-streets-finding-the-groove-with-dave-matthews/.

Welch, Will. "Interview With a Jampire." *CQ*, June 5, 2009. https://www.gq.com/story/interview-with-a-jampire.

Wener, Ben. "Dave Matthews Band's Farewell to a Fallen Brother." *The Orange County Register*, April 20, 2008. https://www.ocregister.com/2008/08/20/dave-matthews-bands-farewell-to-a-fallen-brother/.

Made in the USA
Monee, IL
25 November 2021

83035622R00069